KIM LEGGETT

HOME STORIES

KIM LEGGETT

HOME STORIES

DESIGN IDEAS FOR MAKING A HOUSE A HOME

PRINCIPAL PHOTOGRAPHY BY LESLIE BROWN

ABRAMS, NEW YORK

CONTENTS

INTRODUCTION

CHAPTER 1.
OUR STORY

13   First Impressions

21   Memories Served Here

36   The Gathering Place

43   Suite Dreams

48   Once Upon a Dusty Old Attic

55   Vacancy

58   Double Play

CHAPTER 2.
OTHER PEOPLE'S STORIES

67   Labor of Love

74   The Big Blue House

82   Sugar Shack

89   "The 42"

97   Hideout

103   Vintage Crush

108   Once Upon a Time

114   Boldly Stated

CONTENTS

CHAPTER 3.
SHORT STORIES

124 A New Story for Collected
     Pieces
132 Trading Places
140 The Art of a Storied Display
161 Pen Pals

CHAPTER 4.
A STORY
FOR ALL SEASONS

179 Spring
185 Summer
191 Fall
199 Winter

CHAPTER 5.
SHOPPING GUIDE

207 Why Buy Antiques?
209 Shopping Guide

ABOUT THE AUTHOR

ACKNOWLEDGMENTS

INTRODUCTION

Stories. They are all around us, ripe for the picking. When brought into our homes and woven into our lives they expand the footprint of where we've been and who we have become. They remind us of childhood days, family vacations, holiday celebrations, and new life chapters. They comfort us when life delivers rainy days and bring us joy when family and friends connect with us through the stories that we tell. It's only natural to yearn for an emotional connection with and seek harmony in the elements that surround us in our daily lives. Our homes should be put together with affection by our own hands, with the things we believe in and the people we love.

The idea of designing a home with a spirit of originality and imagination is empowering. To break the mold of traditional decorating and throw design rules to the wind takes practice. No doubt it takes a high level of confidence to get there. Mostly it's getting past the fear that your home doesn't look like those of your friends or the images you've seen on social media. A storied home will never look like any other because each will have its own unique story to tell. You may need to untrain your eye, so to speak. When you consistently peruse

Internet sites you are fooling yourself into believing that these images show the correct way to design a home. The next time you go down that rabbit hole, notice how many of the decorated spaces scrolling past the screen are similar. Once you break free of this contrived approach you'll see beauty and possibility in both objects and design that will inspire you to tell your story in a more conversational way.

When I set out to write *Home Stories* it was always my goal to share inspiring ideas through beautiful pictures that spark creativity. But just as much so, I wish for the stories behind the design to inspire your heart, because styling a home with love and intention is what truly separates a storied home from a decorated house. I'm excited to share for the first time our home and our stories. Each piece is special and built around our lives, whether it's of a past or recent memory or told through the history of the collections that we have found along the way.

We all have busy lives. Designing our spaces shouldn't add to the stress. It should be enjoyable and easily accomplished while allowing our stories to take center stage. I think you'll be pleased to find plenty of practical and affordable ideas and projects that can transform a space in a matter of hours or, at most, no more than a few days. While my decorating style is perfectly suited for me, it's not for everyone. For this reason I've included

"Other People's Stories" (page 62), a beautiful chapter celebrating the stories and design in the homes of some of my dearest friends.

In "Pen Pals" (page 161) you'll find the passionate stories told inside the homes of six Instagram pals whose posts inspire me daily. Here you'll also discover design ideas and family projects from my own home that will not only encourage you, but when used to tell your own story, will also leave family and friends eager to create similar traditions in their homes. "A Story for All Seasons" (page 175) takes you through spring, summer, fall, and winter with simple storied ideas to design a home with less fuss and more time to savor each season.

My hope is that no matter where you are at this moment of life, whether it's in your forever home or in transition and dreaming, you'll find a way to tell your story—one that will be retold and cherished for generations to come. And most of all I hope that you gain a feeling of confidence to say, "I can do this."

CHAPTER 1
OUR STORY

OUR STORY

Telling the story of our home means so much to me. Nearly everything brought in and styled within our own house is connected to our lives in a personal way—whether it's the history of the piece itself, or a past or present memory.

I'm excited to share with you the story of a nineteenth-century bookcase that once belonged to a Civil War soldier from my birthplace in Tennessee, a rug lovingly made by the hand of a homeless New Yorker living with AIDS, a collection of keepsakes gathered from family, an antique church sign that brought back fond memories of Sunday morning church services, and the surprise ending to a story of the time I convinced David to painfully sit through a Broadway musical.

I'm especially proud to share ideas for making a house a home; such as how I transformed my dream farm table into an unexpected arrangement that precisely suits my family, and how a guest bedroom became a shared office space that works beautifully.

Gosh, there's just so much to tell! So, let's get started, shall we?

→ The straight, simple lines of the Odd Fellows lodge chair salvaged from Upstate New York make for a perfect perch to put on and take off shoes. It fit my city cowboy, David, just fine for pulling on his boots. Don't be fooled by the pretty picture though; it doesn't usually look this way. Most days it's a catch-all for bags, hats, jackets, and other articles of clothing.

FIRST IMPRESSIONS

The entryway sets the stage for what is to come and is the introduction to your home's story. Whether it's a grand entrance or a space no larger than a welcome mat, there's plenty you can do to make an impact.

This entryway pairing of a handmade rug and chest began when I spotted the gorgeous early-1800s chest of drawers in a Smoky Mountain antique shop. I fell hard for its authentic abstract paint decoration. Its maker was not only a craftsman but also a painter, an accomplished artist—one before his time. It felt more like a modern masterpiece than a fancied-up chest of drawers.

No room, including an entryway, is complete without the warm feeling offered by a beautiful rug, and I had purchased the perfect one many months before. Around Thanksgiving, David and I took a weekend getaway to New York City. We took our usual stroll along Broadway and Columbus Avenue, admiring the window displays, visiting our favorite thrift stores, and "picking" the Grand Bazaar NYC flea market. If you have never visited a Housing Works Thrift Shop, put one of them on your next New York City itinerary. Their nonprofit stores benefiting homeless people living with AIDS and HIV are chock-full of everything from high-end antiques to general run-of-the-mill thrift-store finds.

As I stepped through the doorway I noticed several large wall hangings that appeared to be works of art. Turns out they were a display of rugs hung on the wall to protect them from foot traffic. I was particularly drawn to one with alternating lines of creams, browns, and blacks. I lifted the tag to discover that these rugs were handmade by artists in the Weaving Project, a group of homeless women living with HIV and AIDS. Each tag told the story of its rug's talented maker. My rug was lovingly woven by "Amirah" in 2006 from shredded scraps of donated clothing and was called *Winter Moss Spring*. Although it was a blustery November day, my heart melted. I thought about Amirah, wondered if she was keeping warm in winter, and if she had food to eat.

When I found the decorated chest I knew instantly that I would bring the work of these two artists together in my home. I felt their lives paralleled somehow. He, more than 200 years ago, keeping comfortable absent modern conveniences, and she doing the same in a world that offered everything—both masters working with their hands, both undiscovered by the great collectors, both cherished by a storyteller.

In my home the entryway overflows into a small, undefined room. The builder intended it to be an office. Instead, I decided to make it a small library and creative space—a sanctuary for inspiration, planning, storytelling, and escape.

My bookshelves are stocked with titles that run the gamut from interior design to folk art collecting to the classics, but I wanted the space to be more than a book depository. I wanted to surrounded myself with the collections that I cherished the most.

Designing a library in the traditional sense often calls for open shelves lining the walls of the room. But in a storied home something more out of the ordinary is desired—and expected. That's why I threw design rules to the wind in favor of a more conversational version, beginning with an 1800s bookcase that once belonged to a Civil War soldier. I fell in love with it for its impressive folk-art details, expert craftsmanship, and immaculately preserved surface, and just as much for its story.

WHEN JOHNNY COMES MARCHING HOME

On April 9, 1865, twenty-year-old Sargent William Franklin Pierce lay down what had been his uniform throughout eleven battles of the Civil War and began his trek homeward to the one-hundred-acre war-damaged family farm in Obion County, Tennessee. For four years he had been a part of the Company H, 47th Tennessee Infantry Regiment of the Confederate States Army organized at Camp Trenton in Gibson County. His claim to fame was the part he played in the infamous two-day Battle of Shiloh from April 6 to 7, 1862.

Although the war was officially over, Pierce must have felt he was still amid the tragedy. The campaign had taken its toll on West Tennessee farms as soldiers had marched through the fields and trampled crops, often burning what was in their way. Yet Pierce set about rebuilding the family homestead, mending fences, and planting crops. The farm was declared a Tennessee Century Farm, a designation given to those continuously farmed by a single family for more than one hundred years.

→ I love how this contemporary space now feels like an old library. The antique New England tilt-top tea table in original black paint was a steal at $75 and now holds the antique Bible collection I had stored away in cardboard boxes for years.

← A unit of shelves should hold so much more than books. It can also serve as a perfect spot to intermingle keepsakes from family travels, special mementos, family photos, and children's artwork among favorite design and reference books. One of my most prized collections is these memory jars. They are a constant reminder of good times spent with our family. We never leave our walks along the seashore without collecting a sand bucket full of shell fragments.

CREATE A TINY LIBRARY ANYWHERE IN YOUR HOME

Whether you have an entire room or a cozy nook, a library should be a personal space. Think of it as a place to intermingle "priceless only to you" family collections. Start by making your bookcase or shelf a focal point. Stray from the traditional by searching out an unexpected vintage or antique piece such as the Civil War bookcase, a china cabinet, or cupboard. Because these types of pieces were often passed down through families, they may come with a story to add to your own. With an antique piece you will want to make sure that the shelves can support the weight of books. Never choose a piece with glass shelving for a bookcase.

NEW TWISTS ON OLD TRADITIONS

In our family, it's a tradition to draw names for Christmas gifts. One year, our little granddaughter Giuliana came up with the sweet idea that instead of buying a gift, we should do something nice that didn't cost money. There were a lot of heartfelt gestures that Christmas Eve, in the form of handwritten notes of love to the guys doing dishes. Our daughter Andrea took a creative approach in thanking David for the love he had shown throughout her life, creating a dozen handwritten personal messages on construction paper and placing them in a large jar. Beginning that day, David selected one note to read and continued the ritual for each of the eleven days that followed. The hand-crafted style of the notes and loving sentiments brought the messages to life and smiles to the whole family.

SAY GRACE

The invitation came by way of a tiny little voice: "Mammie and Pawpaw, will you come to Thanksgiving dinner with me at my school?" It was passionately delivered with sparkling eyes and a crooked-tooth grin—an invitation no grandparent could refuse. The decorations on the dinner tables told the story of the first Thanksgiving, with Pilgrim hats handmade from coffee cans and colorful fall leaves cut from construction paper. It was a huge gathering, with little feet scurrying to find a seat so families could all celebrate together. I wondered if for some this would be the only Thanksgiving meal they would enjoy this season. A little red-haired boy sat across from us, alone and quiet. We asked him to join our family. In our hearts we felt the reason for the season and were thankful that we could be a part of this little life that means so much to us. Before we scooted away, I picked up a red paper leaf and carried it carefully in my hand. It would be a memory of this moment.

It hangs on my wall in glory, displayed in an oversized frame that preserves the story of this time together. There will never be a monetary value to the small, framed piece of paper, but in our family's story it is priceless.

In your own home, don't overlook mementos: a treasured child's drawing or a souvenir from a special celebration can take center stage in a room. Try exaggerating the frame or using a unique mounting technique to create your own heirloom. Framed keepsakes—like our special paper leaf—look great on gallery walls or as a stand-alone masterpiece.

← Something as simple as a child's naïve drawing from a family celebration—like this treasured paper leaf (facing page) in our library—can become the inspiration for a room.

MEMORIES
SERVED HERE

Just past the library our home expands into an open floor plan that includes the dining and family rooms. I like to believe that these building arrangements were meant to encourage togetherness. At least it does in our house.

The dream of a long farm table stretched across my dining room has always been at the top of my wish list. In my mind I painted a Norman Rockwell picture of our family eating home-cooked meals, celebrating birthdays and holidays, sharing stories, and making lifelong memories. I planned it to take on double duty as a worktable too—a makeshift desk and a place for creating projects and crafting with the kids.

The open floor plan of this house offered the first opportunity for that. Its placement fell in front and center of two large double windows that lit up the room even on rainy days. But somewhere within this fantasy I imagined how a long table would eventually play out in my daily kitchen life. Would I end up heaping piles of chaotically organized papers and magazines on one end? Likely so! Or would it be an awkward playing field for a card game for four? Perhaps. In real life maybe this was more of a pipe dream than a reality. But, as with most dreamers, I couldn't toss it up to pure imagination.

I was on a fruit tea run at the fall Columbus, Ohio, Country Living Fair when just outside a vendor's booth I spotted twin sawbucks oddly placed end to end to form a continuous table. Pam (the vendor) spun a tale of their former starring role as tavern dining room tables in the colorful life of Steamboat Landing, a lodge on the Adirondacks' Blue Mountain Lake. With my imagination reading between the lines, I filled in the blanks with all that she had forgotten or never really knew, about the spirited good times and tall tales of the vacationers who had spent summers there. I imagined the many beer mugs raised in toast by overzealous fishermen to "the one that got away," the gossip of the finely dressed city ladies sipping wine as they waited to board the steamboat, and the giggles of sun-kissed teenagers enjoying the lodge's sandy beach just outside their door.

→ It's simple to create your own potting table for an indoor garden using common plumber's pipe and found materials, such as reclaimed wood.

Seeing the two tables placed end to end that day inspired me to create an arrangement for my dining space that was unconventional yet suited my needs. I would join them together for the long-table Norman Rockwell fantasy, then separate them for the bill paying, crafting projects, and games with the kids. It was a design plan I had borrowed from the lodge itself. Tables in restaurant dining are frequently joined together and separated, depending upon seating needs: This seemed like the perfect solution for the Leggett family,

too. The size and ease of transition (pictured at left) offered more dining and entertaining options, like moving them outdoors for lawn parties and alfresco dining.

Just beyond the dining table's edge, a handmade potting table constructed from plumber's pipe and a Franklin, Tennessee, bowling alley floor holds a vintage F. W. Woolworth Company penny toy display, now repurposed for an indoor herb garden. Its dividers seemed custom-made for planting seedlings, but, of course, it has a story of its own.

BACK WHEN EVERY DAY SEEMED LIKE CHRISTMAS

We can thank Mr. Frank Woolworth for the brilliant idea of creating displays that allowed customers to handle products without the help of a salesclerk. Before the F. W. Woolworth Company, most small items sold in a mercantile store were displayed on the store's tall back bars, and it was the storekeeper's job to pass the merchandise across the counter for the customer to examine. But Mr. Woolworth knew the magical power of holding and admiring an object firsthand, particularly if it was a toy.

His beautiful mahogany counters with thick iridescent green glass dividers held everything from beauty products to household items, but I'm pretty sure everyone's favorites were the toys. As a child, it seemed to me the displays were an endless sea of glass. I thought that he must have employed hundreds of elves who worked tirelessly by night because each divider was always filled to the brim with glass marbles, ball and jacks, spinning tops, toy soldiers, dolls made of rubber and dressed in lace from the cutting-room floor, and windup yellow chicks at Easter (my favorite). The glass sections were low enough to allow for easy reach for little ones, but the displays above held the more expensive prizes.

↗ While the outdoorsy vibe from the plants brightens my spirits, my "garden trophies" are among my most loved collections. A vintage cast-iron owl candle lantern watches over the garden on his makeshift perch crafted from a discarded wooden potholder, and the Mary Poppins look-alike—once a cottage weather vane—has become a playful garden ornament.

→ The prize of the display is the handmade antique Victorian birdhouse created entirely from tin. Made by an expert tinsmith, every detail is exquisite and not commonly expected for a simple piece of yard art. From the rising gothic porticos and arched windows to the miniature scale of a cupola, no architectural detail was left unnoticed. I imagine it was once a fancy nesting spot for a momma bird and her babies in spring.

SIMPLE IDEAS FOR USING EVERYDAY KITCHEN ESSENTIALS AS ART

Utilitarian kitchen essentials can serve up much more than the potatoes and gravy. When collected in interesting arrangements they make for beautiful art displays too.

I stumbled upon these pretty pastel bowls while strolling the aisles of the City Farmhouse Popup Fair a few years back. The sun was especially bright that morning and the bowls caught both the light and my attention. I imagined them together in an artful stack. And while my eye is drawn to their timeworn beauty, it's the memories that surround these pieces that ultimately reeled me in.

AN APPLE "PICKIN'" STORY

Back in the day, bowls like these were a necessity for mixing, shelling peas, holding seasonal fruit, and just about anything that was required for daily meals. My great-grandmother Mammie had one on her kitchen table. I don't remember if it had a pastel tint, but I do remember that it held country apples. (You know the kind—spotted and imperfect all over. Not pretty like the grocery store kind. Aren't those the best, though? That crisp first bite with juice running down your chin.) The stubby little tree grew just past the back screen door where its branches almost met the porch. An empty bowl meant that I could pick my own—if I could sneak past those pesky yellow jackets that seemed to forever stand guard over the largest fruits. The sting came without fair warning and left me running, usually with the tightly fisted apple in tow. If I had paid the price, I certainly planned on taking home the prize.

Both Momma (my grandmother) and Mammie (her mother) had plenty of family home remedies for treating most anything that came my way, including yellow-jacket stings. Back then it was quite common for a southern country lady to dip a little snuff—not very ladylike, I know, but a quick remedy to have on hand for taking away the sharp sting of those annoying apple soldiers.

While the bowls will always bring back fond memories of country apples on Mammie's kitchen table, it's more the memory of the snuff paste that turned my head, and my nose, in an upward p-u!

← As if collecting the stone-ware bowls isn't enough, I also have a love for the worn and weathered wooden kind. The good news is, if you are thinking of starting a bowl collection, these 1950 to '60s wood types are less expensive and easier to find than the ironstone and pottery examples. I've had a fondness for these vintage salad bowls that goes waaaay back. It all began with my Aunt Sue, as a lot of my memories often do. Why as a child would I ever notice, or care, that she had more wooden salad bowls than the local five-and-dime? Could it be that I was drawn to patinated wood even then? Her over-varnished pine shelves held hordes of them ranging in all sizes, forms, and colors, but the worn natural ones were the ones I loved most.

→ Woodenware comes
in handy for all sorts of
creative ideas, from serving
up cake and ice cream at
birthday parties to snacks
for the kids.

WORTH THE TRIP

It was lunch at the F. W. Woolworth Co.'s diner counter on our occasional Saturday shopping trips that spawned my interest in collecting restaurant ware. I always looked forward to those outings as it was the only time my family ever dined in a restaurant. Momma cooked all the family meals at home, from scratch. So, sliding into a booth and ordering a "very special" hamburger from a printed menu was a huge treat for this small-town girl. Momma's burgers didn't come with a huge slice of brilliant red tomato, although she grew exactly the same kind in her backyard garden.

She also didn't top hers with fancy curly lettuce or smother the plate with crispy crinkle fries (ours were the homemade kind). The F. W. Woolworth Co. lunch counter potatoes were cut long and cooked golden and served with the best ketchup that money could buy, or so I thought. My meal always arrived on a thick white plate banded in green and bearing the cursive script of the Woolworth's logo. To me, those were the most beautiful plates—not only how they looked, but also the noise they made as they clanked against each other in the busy diner. I once wrote in my childhood diary that my dream was to own the F. W. Woolworth Co.'s plates. Looking back, it was more about the experience, and the plates connected me to it.

→ While stacks of bowls make any kitchen shine, plates can create a similar showing, especially when they are a collection of restaurant ware displayed in an antique cupboard. Often found at flea markets and thrift stores, many of these commercial-use plates bear interesting motifs from their dining establishments. They are heavy-duty, serviceable, and as durable for outdoor dining as they are for indoor everyday use.

ALL SET

Throughout my picking journeys I've never found the Woolworth's restaurant ware I dreamed about, but on an unusually cold fall day in Georgia, at the Country Living Fair, I fell in love with a collection (page 30, 31, and facing page) that I'm sure will grace our family's Thanksgiving table for generations to come. Here was everything needed to serve a feast to a family of twelve, restaurant style! The large collection of cereal bowls, dinner plates, meat platters, and bread plates came with the logo of the Green Ridge Turkey Farm, featuring an image of a hefty boastful turkey. George and Grace Kimball's New England Farm Restaurant opened in 1931 and was best known for its "drawn and ready for the oven" turkeys, and later for fresh sandwiches served to the many tourists who passed along the Daniel Webster Highway route in Nashua, New Hampshire. Sadly, a fire destroyed the farm around Thanksgiving in 1950.

← Alongside the restaurantware, a vintage compote shaped like a gobbler holds cranberry sauce. The antique cast iron skillet that once belonged to Momma serves up a southern Thanksgiving tradition, Chicken and Dressing.

OVEN TIME AND TEMPERATURE CHART		
SWITCH ON BAKE		
BREAD		
BISCUITS	450° F	10-15 MINUTES
MUFFINS	425°	20-25 MINUTES
QUICK LOAF BREAD	375°	60-75 MINUTES
YEAST BREAD, 2-4 LOAVES	400°	50-60 MINUTES
YEAST ROLLS	425°	15-25 MINUTES
CAKE		
ANGEL OR SPONGE	325°	50-60 MINUTES
CUP	375°	20-30 MINUTES
GINGERBREAD	350°	30-40 MINUTES
LAYER, 8 INCH	375°	25-30 MINUTES
LAYER, 8 INCH, CHOCOLATE	350°	30-40 MINUTES
LOAF	350°	45-60 MINUTES
COOKIES		
BROWNIES	325°	35-40 MINUTES
DROP	375°	10-15 MINUTES
ROLLED OR SLICED	375°-400°	10-12 MINUTES
PASTRY		
PUMPKIN PIE	400°	40-50 MINUTES
PIE SHELL	450°	12-15 MINUTES
PIE MERINGUE	325°	15-20 MINUTES
TWO-CRUST PIE	400°	45-55 MINUTES

MEATS		MINUTES PER POUND		
BEEF, STANDING RIB		RARE	MEDIUM	WELL DONE
3-5 LBS.	325°	25-30	30-35	35-45
6-8 LBS.	325°	18-22	22-26	28-33
ROLLED RIB	325°	ADD 10-15 MINUTES PER POUND TO ABOVE.		

CHUCK OR RUMP		
3-5 LBS.	325°	40-45 MINUTES PER LB.
6-8 LBS.	325°	25-30 MINUTES PER LB.
LAMB OR VEAL		
3-5 LBS.	325°	30-40 MINUTES PER LB.
PORK—FRESH		
3-5 LBS.		
SMOKED TENDERED HAM	350°	40-50 MINUTES PER LB.
6 LBS.	325°	18-20 MINUTES PER LB.
10-12 LBS.	325°	10-15 MINUTES PER LB.
POULTRY		
CHICKEN, 4-5 LBS.	325°	35-40 MINUTES PER LB.
TURKEY, 10 OR LESS LBS.	325°	20-25 MINUTES PER LB.
10-15 LBS.	300°	20-22 MINUTES PER LB.
FISH		
WHOLE—4 LBS.	400°	10-12 MINUTES PER LB.

REFER TO INSTRUCTION BOOK FOR BROILING OR USE OF TIMER

MORE FUN WAYS TO TELL YOUR STORY USING EVERYDAY ESSENTIALS

↑ Possibly the most underappreciated, seldom-used cookware is the lowly broiler pan. Every modern stove came equipped, free of charge, with this two-piece grilling sensation. Made of a slotted grate and a drip pan, which collected valuable juices from meats, most broiler pans were plain black or gray and without decoration. However, somewhere along the production line, one innovative stove manufacturer came up with the brilliant idea to imprint a temperature chart onto the drip pan. If it wasn't going to play a part in Suzy Homemaker's meal preparation, it could at least make itself useful as a baking guide. This stroke of genius never sees the inside of my oven, but it serves me well sitting right beside my stove, where it functions as a resting place for my cooking utensils.

↓ Have a soft spot for aged linens? Assemble a stack of dish towels (I prefer the worn ones) alongside a tower of rough-hewn breadboards to create an old-world moment in the kitchen.

↑ Who says a lack of funds can keep a cook from having a full set of knives? In times past (and even today), families created everything from utensils to furnishings for the home using materials on hand in the toolshed or barn. Whenever there was a household need, family handymen (or women) put their self-taught skills to the test and crafted what was needed. The purpose wasn't usually purely aesthetic. Crafted simply from blocks of wood and thin metal, these chopping essentials served one family well over the years. Today they make an interesting folk-art collection displayed on my grandmother's cutting board.

THE GATHERING PLACE

It's not uncommon for the family room to become an extension of the dining area. In our family we don't wait for holidays to get together over a good meal and storytelling. It happens on most weekends, actually. After the meal, the kids hang out on the sofa, and the grown-ups linger around the table for home-made dessert and coffee. The conversation is always spirited, sprinkled with "remember whens" and new tales to tell.

Suppose a furniture piece with a graphic display that allows for a play on words can become a part of those conversations. When I found the antique apothecary at a Franklin, Tennessee, antique shop, it carried a hefty zinger of a price tag. Once I got past the sting, I set a plan in action to own it. That meant a rare opportunity to pass along for a little chump change the "I'll never part with this" collection of the best old wooden signs that I've ever owned. But when you suffer from antique apothecary lust, something's got to give. It's times like these when it's helpful to have a friend whose collecting addiction runs as deep as your own. My sidekick, Lisa, was much obliged to take the prized stash off my hands.

All in all, it's been well worth the trade, because the old drugstore piece from jolly old London has been one of the most fun pieces I've owned. Every four-lettered holiday sentiment (like "July" and "star" for the Fourth of July) has been strung across the top four-drawer slots, and the top gets decorated with vintage finds of the season. But it's not just for seasonal play. The kids created a game called Spelling Wars; whoever can spell the most words in four letters wins the prize—which is nothing more than bragging rights.

→ July ushers in one of my family's most celebrated holidays, Independence Day, and it seemed only fitting that antique flags would be the "stars" of the show. Alongside the tattered quilt, a post–Civil War flag teams up with the star-spangled banners and a patriotic pencil drawing from one of our most trea-sured collected artists, our granddaughter Giuliana.

THREE CHEERS FOR OLD GLORY

Old flags are one of my favorite things to collect and display. Whether it's the tried-and-true red, white, and blue or a variation thereof, nothing tells the story of America's past quite like a flag. If you are lucky enough to scoop one up from a private collector or estate sale it may come with a tall tale to boot. A flea market find like mine often leaves no clues about its previous owner, but history tells us it's in the stars—on the canton that is. The number of stars on a U.S. flag is a sign of its approximate age. For each state added to the Union, a star was added to the flag. The origin or purpose of these particular banners has never been found. But we suspect that they are a symbol of national unity, simply called the "union."

← According to my grandmother, the name of the red rose that bloomed on the massive bush just outside our window around Mother's Day is called the Old Rose. Fact or legend, the name stuck with me. How lucky to have had a fiery display just outside our door for the occasion. Andrea embroidered the sentiment, *"I love you Mom, Andy"* on a piece of snow white cotton cloth when she was just eight years old. When it's not hanging in its permanent spot on my wall, it becomes the centerpiece of the day that honors mom.

A COLOR STORY

Perhaps I was feeling a little frisky the day I decided to spread a riot of color across my white slipcovered sofa. It had long been my ambition to step outside my comfort zone of neutrals and try something new. After twenty-five years of off-white (with the only hint of color being a pale gray), the change was dramatic. I loved it, but had I gone too far?

To ease into the transition, I started with accessories that would be simple to change—pillows and a rug. I began with the rug, since this would be the largest footprint of new color in the room. It's difficult to make a final decision when you can't see the rug in your space. Most rug stores will allow approvals, so taking home a selection of various sizes, shades, and patterns will help make your buying decision easier.

A nice selection of pillows in various patterns and colors came from a local big-box store, which are easier on the wallet than specialty shops and less difficult with returns. To play it safe, I stuck with tried-and-true off-white pillows as a canvas for the bold colors I layered on the sofa. Then I added a couple of foundation solids in orange and blue, accenting the colors found in the rug and patterned pillows as well as in the blue of the nineteenth-century painted strongbox that I had repurposed as a coffee table. Surprisingly, it was the patterned pillows that sealed the deal for me, reminding me of an abstract painting and giving the sofa an art-like vibe.

My advice is to live with a major design change for at least a couple of weeks, but don't linger. Once you commit to it, it's easier to move on and put any doubts to rest.

SUITE DREAMS

If you're like me, designing the master bedroom can be a real challenge. It's a place where mistakes are made and dreams are born. An oxymoron, I know, but gosh it's so true. It is the one space you want to look pretty and sloppy all at the same time. You design a beautiful bed covering but then don't make the bed. You choose a handy chair or bench for putting on your shoes but then scatter piles of clothes across it. After a long busy day, wouldn't we all like to drift off in a comfortable, uncluttered space?

The biggest obstacle to a welcoming bedroom is trying to put too much in a room that's meant to be calming. Once I realized that, it didn't take long to design a cozy, restful spot.

First choose a comfortable bed. The size that you select will determine the scale of the rest of the furnishings. Our master has a king-size bed and is a typical builder-grade size of 225 square feet. To conserve space, I chose to forgo a traditional headboard and footboard, opting instead for a simple bed frame. An antique French chalkboard-turned-headboard serves as a striking substitute, as well as an uncommon wall decoration.

TIME TRAVELER

The French chalkboard was a road trip find when we made a pit stop near a thrift store in Amarillo, Texas, a few summers ago. Back in Paris, the old notice board had served a café proprietor well, offering up the daily menu at a busy sidewalk café. Age and the open air had pitted and worn its smooth writing surface, and its once brilliant shade of emerald green had given way to a mellow patina that now resembled the weathered verdigris, of Parisian copper rooftops. Its new life as a stowaway seemed everlasting—that is, until a biologist rescued it for a classroom exhibit on the study of nature.

When it eventually made its way to the States, time had erased nearly all the chalk-drawn illustrations, although a ghostly dragonfly and a Christmas beetle seemed to have crawled to the edge to escape their extinction. The tiny feather floating at the bottom edge of the board offered a calming feeling, so I thought it should stay. I had my artist friend Erin chalk out a larger version to center and lighten the whole scene.

ABOUT THAT DUMPSTER DIVE IN NEW YORK CITY . . .

After twenty-two years of marriage, many trips to New York City, and countless hours of encouragement, I convinced David to sit through a Broadway musical. It was the last call of *Finding Neverland*, a stellar show that brought to life the fascinating story of how Peter became Pan. But though it was the end of the run for the show in New York, perhaps unsurprisingly it wouldn't be the final curtain for one Neverland memento.

Have you ever wondered what goes on after the run of a live theatrical performance? To witness a show being dismantled, packed up, and moved from the theater is a performance all its own. Hundreds of black trunks cradling everything from costumes, makeup, lighting, and sound equipment are loaded onto large trucks and taken to a warehouse to be stored until the show opens in another city (or country in some instances). It was interesting to watch it all unfold, but I was distracted by the monstrous forty-foot dumpster that sat alongside the moving vans. Discarded cardboard boxes, paper posters, and the usual trash were flung from the doors into the open receptacle. Thanks to David's keen "pickin'" eye, he spotted a side table used as a prop being tossed into midair toward the dumpster. Although he was reluctant, I encouraged him to go in for a dive. "Do it, just do it," I nervously whispered. At that moment the union manager stepped beyond view of the dumpster and David jumped in and snagged the prize. No time to grab, tuck, and run. It was a table for crying out loud! On the surface it was nothing special, just a common 1930-ish side table that most homes had during the Depression. But to me it was spectacular, and it was going home with us thanks to the hotel, which offered a shipping service for tourists who either bought too much or just happened to go on a dumpster dive while visiting the city. By the way, David loved the show.

← Many design mistakes start with furnishings that are too large for the space. By nature, bedroom storage pieces can be large and bulky and look out of scale. Opt instead for a chest of drawers with simple form and graceful lines. We were lucky to find this early nineteenth-century chest on stand in a Franklin, Tennessee, antique shop. The open framework fools the eye into thinking that the chest takes up less space than it does. Above it hangs an antique trade sign. Its worn black surface speaks more to a modern work of art than to its original purpose as an advertisement for a New York florist.

SIMPLY SOUTHERN

In nineteenth-century America, every home, whether a sprawling plantation or small farmhouse, had a blanket chest. Storage space was sparse, so the rectangular box, usually on legs, was necessary for tucking away blankets, quilts, and other bedding. This handsome example dating to the early 1800s was found in a barn on one of the earliest farms in Williamson County (Franklin, Tennessee). Established in 1799, the farm has an aged yellow sign in front of the brick one-story home marking its long standing in the community and its designation as a Century Farm.

Humble storage pieces like this one, crafted in classic country form and retaining their original dry surfaces, are prized by Americana collectors. Today, it serves the same purpose in my bedroom as it did more than 200 years ago.

ONCE UPON
A DUSTY OLD ATTIC

Many of us look at our attics with their sloping ceilings and tucked-away places and think, "This would make a great bedroom." David and I did when we designed a spare room above our garage. I envisioned a cozy space filled with my special collections: an antique iron bed, a yard-long photograph, and, my favorite, the antique wooden Baptist Church sign that I found in Memphis, Tennessee.

That old country-church sign brought back so many memories for me. I was born and raised Southern Baptist. Every week, without fail, my grandmother took me to Sunday school followed by "preaching" at the Second Baptist Church in Dyersburg, Tennessee. I sat beside my younger cousin, Kelley, and our snickering was frowned upon by Momma, who offered more in pinches than she did in praise at the Sunday morning services. Our small congregation was made up mostly of the surrounding Mill Town neighborhood where everyone knew everyone—and everyone's business. For us, getting there was just a walk halfway around the block or a shortcut through the neighbor's backyard. Our entire family belonged to that church—aunts, uncles, and cousins. Revivals were big back then and out-of-town guest preachers ran the gamut from hotshot big-city boys to country charmers.

Had it not been for my mother taking over the master bedroom on an extended visit, I would not have experienced the cozy vibe of the attic bedroom firsthand. It had been our sleeping quarters for a month. That meant nights in the antique iron bed that had once traveled to our granddaughter Lila's house but had found its way home again. Turns out it just wasn't cool enough for a teenager. I was grateful though. I had always loved its graceful lines and cast decoration. The trouble with old beds is that they were produced in only three sizes— full or regular, twin, and three-quarter—making it tight for most statures, like David at six-foot-four. I heard his feet clang the footboard on many restless nights. He said it felt like sleeping in a tree house.

ONE MAN'S TRASH

The wall decorations around the bed speak literally of the Old South. The directional road sign that reads "SOUTH" was a sweet find in a drainage ditch along an Indiana back road. It perfectly described the yard-long photograph—a gathering of the "Southwide Baptist Training Union in Ridgecrest, North Carolina, on July 18–23, 1937." Tennessee, Alabama, Mississippi, and Georgia make up a big part of the Bible Belt, so you can bet any time these fine, devout, Southern church folk had the opportunity to "go to meeting" there was going to be a tribe. Southern Baptists aren't just about religion, mind you. These Protestants played a strong role in politics and society way before American writer and

satirist H. L. Mencken coined the term *Bible Belt* in 1925. Outside the South, Southern Baptists were looked upon as "very religious," and that suited them just fine. The photograph didn't quite fit the unusually substantial frame, but that didn't stop some proud Baptist from showing off their meeting memory in style— nothing that a little cardboard around the edges couldn't fix.

GOING TO
THE CHAPEL AND
WE'RE GONNA
GET MARRIED

When David and I married in April of 1995, he was proudly sporting a mullet haircut. I'm convinced that it's truly unforgettable, or a good laugh, because our social-media friends look forward to the anniversary post of our wedding day photograph every year.

A few months before the wedding we had opened a large antique mall, and that left us little time for prenuptial planning. So we decided to elope just up the road, to the Great Smoky Mountains. Being a couple that wanted to forego commercial wedding chapels for a little country church, we decided to take a drive through the winding mountain back-roads to look for one. Soon we came upon a picturesque chapel nestled in the clearing of a grove of trees. A house sat next door and, as it is with most country churches, the pastor and his wife lived there. (I suppose the congregation feels it necessary to have the preacher near his flock in the event a confession couldn't wait until Sunday morning, or a couple head over heels in love wants to tie the knot on the fly.) A knock on the door produced an elderly man who, just as I was about to give him that "let's pretend this never happened" look, asked, "How can I help you?" My request was

nervously delivered with a rambling explanation of how David and I loved the setting of his little country church and would like to be married there right away—meaning that day! The astonished look on his face soon gave way to a large grin. "What's the rush?" he asked. Turns out he had just returned from the hospital for the removal of a painful kidney stone, so he kindly asked if we could postpone the "I dos" until the following day. As you know, we did.

PRETTY IN PINK

My grandmother (Momma) always said that pink wasn't my color. Every Easter I dreamt of being all dressed up in a Sunday frock the color of cotton candy, but usually mine was a light-blue ruffled dress layered with a sheer white pinafore. Perhaps that's why my favorite shirt is a pink-and-white striped thrift store find, and why I fell so in love with this chest of drawers. The old piece had gone through a restoration (due to neglect over the last hundred years). My friend Heather, who rescued it, thought that its diminutive size was perfect for a little girl's room, so she decided to paint it pink. When I saw it I knew I had to own it. Its scale was a perfect fit for an oddly angled attic ceiling. The buffalo-check chair was a big-box-store find. I do step out of my vintage and antique comfort zone on occasion, especially when I find a piece in one of my favorite classic upholstery patterns.

← This dresser top has been restyled at least a dozen times. Each makeover is usually composed in layers and with collections that I'm particularly fond of. I found this 1800s cabinet card photo at an antique mall, and although it was torn and stained with age, it stole my heart. The mother and child appear to be posing along a sunny beach, yet they aren't at the beach at all. Once backdrops for photography became popular, studios in seaside towns offered beach views of nearby resorts. I like to imagine it was taken at Coney Island. Layered with a hand-stenciled Ohio quilt pattern painted on board by my friend, Katie, and a collection of string balls, it's a nice refresh when I'm longing for a change.

← For years, vintage clocks have appealed to home decorators as a simple nostalgic way to decorate a bookcase or shelf, or to build into collections. I was drawn to this particular 1965 model because of the name Gabriel in script along the clock face. There's a guardian angel in the Bible named Gabriel, and who couldn't use one of those by your slumbering side? It's a sweet sentiment and perfect for my hotel-themed guest room.

VACANCY

Guest bedrooms come together in mysterious ways. But the idea of guests and travelers brought the image of hotels to mind. Besides, I happened to have a stellar collection of antique and vintage hotel pieces on hand, and I thought it would be fun to design a room around them. Maybe too many nights on the picking trail makes me giddy for old hotels—oftentimes it's the doors on these old establishments that draw me in more than the decor.

While a franchise hotel may offer more amenities, I find myself searching out spots with a past. It was "standing on the corner in Winslow, Arizona," and breakfast at the historic La Posada hotel that gave me the idea to recreate an old boardinghouse room in my guest bedroom. While some of these establishments are plain Jane, others were designed with bold colors or large-patterned wallpaper. To create a contemporary version, I searched for and found the perfect wallcovering online. It's more boho style than an old-fashioned pattern, but it offers a huge dose of nostalgia. Its busy, bright colors play beautifully against the nineteenth-century French brass hotel bed that I found at a local flea market for a mere eighty bucks.

→ The antique hotel key bank was a pick many moons ago and while I had at first planned to keep it, I ended up selling it to a friend. I always say though that if something is meant to be yours it will come back to you. Just so happened, when I was looking for pieces to design the guest room, my friend asked if I wanted to buy it back. The primitive keys and drawers for ten rooms are the giveaway that it wasn't hanging in a Hilton.

← The weathered turquoise door, found just outside of Dallas on a picking trip, was the inspiration for the room. I like to imagine the stories told behind those old closed doors when the wild, wild West was young. Did famed outlaws Bonnie and Clyde sleep there? Legend has it that the Dallas-Fort Worth area hotels were the duo's frequent haunts, where they hid from the law, cased out banks, and once jumped from a second-story window to evade capture. I can just see Clyde having a good laugh over yet another eventful escape, and Bonnie spit-shining her boots while recounting stories of how they left the sheriff in a trail of dust.

ROOMS

DOUBLE PLAY

What happens when the inspiration for a tiny home office is a colorful blanket? You end up with a multifunctional space. The bold pattern of oranges, indigos, yellows, and browns of the 1940s Mexican wedding blanket was meant to be shown off, not tucked away in a closet. So I designed a room around it. Now the space doubles as a camp-style sleeping quarters and a home office.

If you are wondering how my desk looks so neat and tidy, it's because the mess usually takes place at one end of my kitchen table. This so-called workspace is upstairs, and I don't care for the quiet vibe. Funny thing, but distraction inspires me—the chatter of people in a room and the background noise of the TV. Being one who doesn't want any space to go to waste, I decided to double up on this room's function. It's especially tiny, only 100 square feet, so it was important that the furnishings stay functional as well as stylish.

Using a wall-mounted desk was a smart decision for the work area. Its open construction contributes to a sense of spaciousness and light. Originally a workbench in a barn, this piece is made of reclaimed oversized antique corbels and an old discarded barn door, easily found at most flea markets and salvage yards. It's a simple piece to recreate. New materials from a home improvement store can offer the same function and effect. Just paint and distress the contemporary alternative for a more vintage look.

↑ The pride and joy of my tiny workspace, as well as a great conversation piece, is the nineteenth-century trade sign that hangs as a focal point over the desk. Before any words are ever spoken there is laughter and finger pointing at the misspelled word—paper. I wonder if the decorator ever noticed it, or even cared.

→ The twin bed is styled in a 1940s Mexican wedding blanket and is the inspiration piece for the room. It was getting over my fear of using bold colors when styling the sofa in the family room that encouraged me to purchase the blanket to use as a bed covering. Handwoven from hand-dyed wool, the rich tones create a warm, cozy vibe and soften the hard surfaces of the workspace across the way.

A simple art installation (that doubles as a headboard) hangs over the bed. I picked the frame at an Ohio flea market, not knowing its original purpose—and I still don't know today. I was drawn to the natural wood and straight line construction. Household twine attaches the deer antlers to the frame.

↓ An oil on board painted in tribute to a monumental catch by Mrs. F. Warrington Gillet on July 15, 1960, along the Alta River in Norway. Mrs. Gillet snagged a 51-pound eight-year-old male Atlantic salmon measuring 50 inches long with a 26-inch girth. I'm curious if this is actually the one that got away.

CHAPTER 2

OTHER PEOPLE'S STORIES

OTHER PEOPLE'S STORIES

INSPIRING STORIES
FROM THE HOMES OF FRIENDS

I happen to have a passion for many home styles and eclectic decor. While I wouldn't necessarily design my home the way a friend or family member would, I still have an appreciation for the creativity that tells their story. Truth is, I love a home with a personality that is as unique as the family who lives there. From a tiny cottage with a storied past to a boho cabin deep in the woods, from a songwriter's big blue house to a young Swedish girl's love story, come take a front row seat as we tour the homes of some of my dearest friends and get inspired to create your own home's stories.

→ In the master bedroom at Jenni and Jared Bowlin's house (page 102), a period chest-of-drawers grounds a nineteenth-century portrait of a gentleman. The graduated stack of suitcases gathered over many stops along the picking trail becomes an art-like display and a connection to the couple's life on the road. They also come in handy as hidden storage.

LABOR OF LOVE

Built in 1900 as part of Franklin's first historic district of Hincheyville, Katie and Randy Williams's home is constructed on property originally owned by Civil War–era mayor John McEwen. It was McEwen's niece and her husband who raised the home there, and like many historic properties it was eventually purchased as an investment, turned into a rental, and converted into a duplex. Ironically, Katie and Randy were former tenants, and when the landlord offered the property for sale the couple jumped at the chance to restore it to its former glory.

The budget-conscious renovators poured their heart, soul, and a whole lot of elbow grease into the home's revival, salvaging and shining original oak and pine hardwood floors, uncovering period fireplaces, restoring original architectural details, and crafting a modern kitchen. The project has been a true labor of love for the couple whose hope from the beginning was to create a space where guests would

feel cared for. While the meticulous conservator's hand is evident throughout the home, it's Katie's personal design touches entwined with family mementos that tell the story.

Nothing is too common to be highlighted as if it has special meaning. That includes the heartfelt messages, cards, and photos Katie and Randy exchanged weekly during a fourteen-month long-distance courtship (Katie in Texas, Randy in Tennessee). When Katie moved to Tennessee the love letters were stowed in a closet, which somehow didn't feel right. Now they are proudly displayed in an old cracked bowl that reminds the couple of a Leonard Cohen quote: "There's a crack in everything, that's how the light gets in."

← Glass-paned doors modernize a traditional period bookcase. A collection of pottery and books (turned spine-in) maintain the neutral tones of the room.

MUZZY DEAREST

Katie's enduring love for her grandmother is a common thread woven throughout the home. Muzzy, as Katie called her, was an art teacher and a missionary. Her humble callings didn't define her personality; Katie remembers her as a rule breaker and a fiercely independent woman.

While helping Muzzy with spring cleaning, Katie discovered a collection of drawings that had been rolled up for the discard pile. Turns out they were Muzzy's first works, sketched while she was studying art in college. Treated as salvaged masterpieces by Katie, she framed the illustrations and incorporated them into her home's story as a prized collection.

A tiny corner reserved for a quiet reading nook holds more fond memories of Muzzy—that's her in the photo on the left with her sister. The tiny Chinese paper card lovingly propped alongside the picture is actually Muzzy's name written in Mandarin. When Katie was going through her things, she initially threw it away thinking it was scrap paper. Something told her to go back for it. Perhaps it was Muzzy's nudge—Katie feels that she's always nearby.

↑ Combinations of organic textures, patterns, and colors soothe the soul. Green moss fills a large planter on the table, a simple yet sophisticated touch to the space that overlooks layers of natural stone just outside the window.

← In the family room, Muzzy's art takes center stage above a minimal yet comfortable striped bench-sofa. The design helps conserve every inch of space in the intimate family room. The single furniture piece offers more seating and takes up less real estate than a pair of chairs.

→ Who needs Picasso drawings when you can hang the work of your family and friends? They may not be museum-worthy pieces, but they tell a much more personal story. Muzzy's husband—Katie's grandfather, Jim, or Bampa, as Katie called him—had no formal art training, but that didn't stop him from showing his art-teacher "missus" he had talent. He sketched out the "Self Portrait," his first (and final) masterpiece, which hangs in tribute over the bar (actually a marble-top French baker's slab turned drinks-mixing table). The sketch of a chair, Katie's first drawing from her interior design class in college, contributes to the sentimental art display.

Although the kitchen required a complete overhaul, Katie preserved some old-fashioned character by salvaging the original white-oak rafters and using them for rustic shelving. In keeping with the organic vibe, earth-toned and textured dinnerware lines the shelves alongside a collection of handmade tableware, a gift from Katie's friend Joanna who was married in the house. When Katie first saw the ceramics, she was surprised to learn Joanna had made them years before when she was a working potter. Inspired by Joanna's artistry, Katie suggested that she pick up where she left off many years ago. Within days the friends had located a used firing furnace on an online marketplace and traveled together to pick it up. Through Katie's encouragement, Joanna started a business, Particle Ceramics, and her beautiful handmade tableware is now sold around the world.

→ Sticking with the same palette between family room, dining room, and kitchen eases the transition and promotes consistent flow. Large-paned windows installed during the renovation provide the added bonus of ample natural light and make the small space feel larger. Vintage furnishings like the folding farm table and a simple wooden bench for seating provide nostalgic charm, while a pair of clean-lined mid-century chairs offer a modern contrast to the more rustic furnishings.

CREATE THE
ILLUSION OF SPACE

Shaker-style cabinetry keeps the kitchen's mood airy. Glass doors on upper cabinets reflect light and create a greater sense of openness and space. The eye is naturally drawn to the highest contrasting point in a room, which in a kitchen is usually the open space above the cabinets. Leaving this area open can create the feeling that the walls are shorter than they actually are. Katie's solution: She installed a furr down, enclosing the area between the ceiling and the top of the kitchen cabinets. This gives the room the illusion of greater height.

↑ Katie didn't forgo a generous work surface because of space restrictions. It was important that the island provide ample counter space for the preparation of meals and for guests to gather around during the process. Isn't that where many spirited conversations begin—in the kitchen? She thoughtfully designed the island to provide extra storage and pull-up seating. In keeping with the crisp aesthetic throughout the space, she chose Bianco Carrara marble as a work surface. Quarried from bedrock in Carrara, Italy, it is one of the many white marbles produced in the area and is more budget friendly than others from the region.

→ A map of Nashville rests atop a dark wood bench, lending contrast and a level of style to the entry. The resting spot transforms the space from pathway to a welcome place to perch.

THE BIG BLUE HOUSE

When a Cali-girl songwriter-turned-aspiring-novelist discovered a big blue house along a southern back road, she packed up her beachy Malibu home for a sprawling two-and-a-half story, twelve-room house nestled in the rolling hills of Leiper's Fork in Franklin, Tennessee. When describing the house to family and friends she affectionately called it "the big blue house," and the name just stuck. It was here that Jamie Parsons rekindled her passion for designing a home that reminds her of childhood days spent with her grandparents scouring antique shops for one-of-a-kind finds.

← Jamie's "room with a view" is a perfect spot to start the day with a cup of coffee. Who could resist all that sunshine pouring in from the large windows?

↓ Facing love seats encourage good conversation and a healthy exchange of stories. Jamie snagged the lush 1920s velvet love seats at auction long before she discovered the Big Blue House.

→ Jamie's collection of antique men's shirt collars and a child's silhouette hang above an 1800s travel trunk. When she found the collars, she had no idea

what they were much less how she would use them. Learning that they were the detachable part of a man's dress shirt, she imagined them worn by bankers, lawyers, and a tuxedo-clad gentleman at a fancy party. After a 2:00 A.M. "punch drunk" decorating frenzy inspired her to hang them on an empty foyer wall, guests and family were drawn to them, leading her to make it a more permanent arrangement. The wicker top hat was found on one of her Saturday antiquing outings. It came without a story, but she found it so unusual she took it home to begin her own.

← In Jamie's music room, vintage guitars aren't just for looks. Guests are encouraged to take one down and pick out a tune or two. The collection includes a 1970s Harmony, a blue resonator (the instruments fashioned with spun-metal cones on the body to pick up string vibration), and a handmade three-string cigar-box guitar. A vintage drum case she picked up at auction was just right for a side table for whiskey sipping. Creative inspiration comes from black-and-white photographs of Jamie's favorite musicians, like Ray Charles and Merle Haggard, the legend of country music who kick-started her love for songwriting.

↓ Furnishing a rambling house takes time and an openness to whimsy. Jamie let pieces that spoke to her win out over those with a stylized look. These vintage school lockers at a Nashville antique store caught her eye. Now they serve as a coat closet and a perch for her collection of cowboy and trucker hats.

← Once Jamie settled in, it didn't take friends and family long to start spinning tales around the 12-foot-long farm table made from reclaimed wood salvaged from a late-1800s mercantile store. A vintage portrait of an elderly woman overlooks the dining room from the mantle and is the most talked-about piece in the house. Maybe it's her quirky expression and granny glasses that are part of the attraction. Vintage portraiture is having a moment—from little old ladies to stone-faced gents, the instant-ancestry trend shows no signs of slowing down. If you're wondering why all the sitters look so grim, it's because back then it was socially unacceptable for a subject to be seen smiling in his or her portrait.

↑ A pretty white-and-indigo patterned cotton tablecloth makes for a striking display when paired with vintage floral china in the same tones and contrasting patterns. Infusing a note of solid color (which rests the eye), the unfussy centerpiece is made using greens cut from Jamie's yard accented with golden pears from the market.

↑ Despite their good looks, antique beds don't always suit modern-day needs. That's when a beautifully crafted copy is better suited. The tall turned posts of a contemporary version better matched the scale of the large master bedroom, and its modern construction offers more comfort for sleeping. In keeping with a simpler time, Jamie preferred the graceful lines of an antique tea table over a traditional nightstand. Adding a patriotic touch is a framed fragment of a vintage American flag, a special gift from a friend.

↓ There's a wonderland of beauty just outside the back door. At the pond, you can kick back with a wicker basket filled with fruity drinks and peanut butter sandwiches. The calm waters of the pond needed life, so Jamie stocked it with fish, who in turn invited over their friends, the frogs and a big ol' turtle. Now if she could just keep the ants from joining the picnic.

SUGAR SHACK

What began in the late 1800s as a railroad section house turned into an award-winning historic preservation project for artist Harrison Houlé and actor husband, John Schuck. The tiny cottage that sits within fifty feet of the railroad tracks was originally owned by the L&N (Louisville and Nashville Railroad) to provide housing for the laborers who worked along the route. When the couple purchased the home in downtown Franklin, Tennessee, its former tenants over the past hundred-plus years had left behind deteriorating floors, decaying rooms, and a shady past. Yet somehow the couple felt a peaceful presence the moment they stepped through the door. That magical feeling convinced them that the cottage should be theirs, and they felt ready to take on the daunting task of bringing it back to life.

Its most infamous occupant was Beulah, an enterprising woman who ran a successful underground moonshine operation from the house during Prohibition. That was until she realized that setting up the illegal sale of alcohol near the middle of town and within easy reach of the long arm of the law was not the best business decision. Her prosperous career ended when she was arrested for the illegal sale of moonshine. Remnants of her "forced to close" operation were discovered beneath the house during the renovation, leading the couple to wonder how many pints could she have possibly stored under the two-room cottage. I'm thinking that with the tracks close by it was a steady stop-n-go for Beulah.

→ Southern country meets French blue in the vintage dining table and chairs, an ideal fit for the small kitchen. In tight dining quarters, opting for a round table over a square or rectangular one creates more space to move about the room. It is a cozy spot for lingering conversations over a cup of coffee or a great meal.

← The star of the family room is an 1800s French cupboard that Harrison discovered in my secret stash at City Farmhouse. Once she made it past the curtain that hid all the "not for sale" goodies, there was no stopping her from taking it home. When she told me it would be the feature story in her little historic cottage, I just couldn't say no. My picker friend Camille had found the piece on a trip to Paris and it was love at first sight when she offered it to me. I was smitten with the expert craftmanship and the fine details created by the hand of a French cabinetmaker more than 150 years ago. Although worn, the original paint is exquisite and is one of the reasons I fall in love with these old pieces.

→ Back in the 1940s in Buffalo, New York, young John was making paper airplanes on the baking table where his grandmother had turned out scrumptious pies decades earlier. Fifty years later he was happy to inherit the table (right), which he turned into a writing desk. Above the table is an oil painted by Harrison following a trip to Ireland, during which she stayed in the early fifteenth-century Luttrellstown Castle on the outskirts of West Dublin. There's nothing like spending a week in a castle to inspire an artist to paint, and the view from her window of the pasture below inspired her to preserve that memory as art. For Harrison the experience was like living in a real-life fairytale with fragrant gardens, rooms fit for a queen, and twenty-four-hour maid service.

← Doors figure largely in the bedroom suite's design. In addition to the refined French entry doors, a rustic barn door, handcrafted by the couple's son, mimics a period version. It pulls double duty, offering privacy for the bathroom and as a work of art for the bedroom. In keeping with the period, Harrison installed a replica of an antique cast-iron soaking tub. In the late nineteenth century, a claw-foot tub was considered a luxury; for some, it still is today. After more than a century, it is still the one fixture whose design marries well with almost any style of home.

← A back porch can't be beat for bringing family and friends together over cool drinks, home-cooked food, and good conversation. In a small space, it's a welcoming extension of the home. To allow for more guest seating, Harrison added an antique mercantile store bench that she freshened up with a coat of white paint.

→ Don't ever place an intentional blank space in front of an artist and expect it to go unadorned. The blank canvas of the inner side of the Sugar Shack's garden gate beckoned Harrison to paint a primitive garden "Mum," inspired by a picture in a French book. She named her "Alice in the Garden" in tribute to the property's first owner.

→ A back-porch swing piled thick with cozy pillows invites you to linger long after a good meal or curl up with a book and catch a breeze on a warm afternoon. Just after sunset you'll want to turn your ear to the song of the whippoorwill. If you're a marriage-minded woman, however, it's best to turn away. Legend has it that if a single woman heard her first whippoorwill call in spring and the bird didn't immediately call again, she would remain a spinster for at least a year. But if she made a wish upon hearing the call, and kept it a secret, a suitor was sure to come her way.

← It's marching orders for a collection of vintage cowboy boots lined up on a primitive jelly cupboard. Once used for storage in a farmhouse kitchen, the antique piece is now a handy stowaway cabinet for mud boots and other gear needed for exploring "the 42."

"THE 42"

A Missouri girl and a Florida boy were happily living the dream in sunny Orlando with their two young girls and three cats when Daniel (the hubby) got the itch to move. Laura (the wife) knew it would have to be somewhere both beautiful and intriguing enough to satisfy his entrepreneurial spirit. She began researching hot spots in Tennessee and soon the couple settled in the countryside of Franklin. The rolling forty-two acres ("the 42" as it's affectionately called) offered room to roam, creeks to explore, old pre-Civil War bridges to cross, and the ideal spot to build their forever home. In 2019 Laura and Daniel made the decision to keep the historic land that they cherish as a forever part of the natural landscape of their state by placing "the 42" in the Land Trust for Tennessee.

With large rooms and unexpected nooks and crannies, the house has plenty of space for Laura to display her collections of vintage finds, including those that she picked when she was only sixteen. Back in Missouri, while most teenagers were going to the shopping malls, Laura and her brother were stalking antique shops, flea markets, and thrift stores. Her love for picking is still her favorite pastime and she has developed a keen eye over the years. The pieces on display are only part of the story. She has a hoard of vintage ironstone, antique landscape paintings, and all other sorts of curiosities stowed away in closets all over the house. For now, she's still considering the possibilities. Steady and sure, that's her goal. Designing a home takes thought if you want to decorate from the heart.

↑ If there's ever a doubt in the couple's minds that their land was a lucky find, they have plenty of natural evidence to reinforce the notion of good fortune. Their meadows abound with four-, five-, and six-leaf clovers. Laura tucks the good luck charms within the pages of a few prized books for safekeeping. The odds of finding even a single four-leaf clover is one in ten thousand!

The old saying about good luck following four-leafers multiplies with five, which indicates attracting money, and six offers the whole enchilada—money, good fortune, love, faith, hope, *and* extra luck. Looks as though Laura is pretty well covered.

→ In the family room, crisp white walls and shiplap ceilings contrast with the natural wooden beams. Built-in bookcases offer a show-and-tell spot for a collection of vintage books, silhouettes, musical instruments, and other collected oddities. Laura, who is a photographer, devised a design solution to hide the "big screen over the mantle." While visiting the scenic Ring of Kerry in Ireland she captured a stunning mountain landscape that is on view on-screen when the television isn't in use.

← An early primitive carved tren-
cher serves as a centerpiece on
the island as well as an attractive vessel for corralling fruit.

RETHINKING THE KITCHEN ISLAND

When Laura was looking to outfit her newly built kitchen with an island, she opted out of the builder's version. Instead, she snagged a vintage industrial cart on a pick at the Nashville Flea Market and asked her cabinetmaker if he could customize a serviceable furniture piece for her kitchen. Using salvaged materials, he outfitted the cart with a row of utensil drawers on each side and added a slab of quartz for a durable countertop. Laura is particularly fond of the lower kettle shelf. Who wants to dig around in cabinets and drawers for cooking vessels?

Since her home is designed with family gatherings and entertaining in mind, Laura chose the classy French Lacanche range for cooking. Handcrafted in Burgundy, the French cook stoves are considered the highest quality both by cooking enthusiasts and professional chefs. The black-painted lower cabinetry provides a deep contrast with the white walls and natural wood accents and gives the large, airy kitchen both sophistication and down-home charm.

In the master bedroom Laura and Daniel must feel like they are living in a landscape painting thanks to two larger-than-life windows that offer a breathtaking view. Even on rainy and cloudy days the natural daylight fills the room. The bedside table is ample and fitting for the large space. Its French heritage likely indicates it began life in a garden or wine tasting room. The base is cast iron and the top is soapstone. If Laura decides to replace it, I think it would make a lovely mixing table.

← The old adage that you should live in a room a while and feel its bones before decorating it is still true. While Laura carefully contemplates her strategy for the formal dining room (as she has done, room by room), a minimal sense of beauty rules the day.

HIDEOUT

Back in his youth Darryl McCreary hammered out a neighborhood of treehouses throughout the woods that surrounded his family home. So it was no surprise that he chose to continue his childhood passion in his adult life. The cabin is the closest you'll come to living in a treehouse, yet with all the amenities of home. The narrow, almost upright path to the door is layered with a thick forest of old-growth trees and opens just barely enough to discover the cabin built with Darryl's own hands on family land. Annie, his better half, set out to design the space in a rustic-boho style that tells the story of her love of family and flea market finds.

↑ Annie's mom, Diane, was a prolific picker. Her heart was in the thrill of the hunt and the stories of the authentic farmhouse finds that she unearthed in barns and homesteads along the rural backroads of Pennsylvania and Virginia. She hauled the prized loot back to her Tennessee farmhouse or passed it along to Annie. The old one-room-schoolhouse bench seemed just the ticket for seating at the family's farm table. It was found on one of Diane's many picks to the country. Annie gave it a good spit-shine and styled it up for comfort using a faux-fur throw and pillows made from vintage ticking and grain sacks.

If your home goals are to wrap yourself in the warmth of a curated space surrounded by your fondest stories, then linger here a bit for endless inspiration. The gallery wall is the highlight of the dining space and features Annie's favorite paintings, all found at thrift stores and flea markets. The collection is both playful and

random and incorporates worn mirrors with special meaningful touches, like the silhouettes of three generations of the McCreary family: Annie's boys, Darryl as a child, and his mom. Antique rugs collected over time by her mother help bring the space to life.

The 1970s Orley woodstove was a local Craigslist score, and its barrel design was the perfect aesthetic for the cabin. The stoves weren't originally intended to be a commercial product. To save on high electric bills during the cold Oregon winters, Orley Milligan made one for the sole purpose of heating his chainsaw store. Soon customers were impressed, and Orley set up production in the back room. Although thousands were made and sold, it is uncommon to find one that has traveled this far from the West Coast. To beef up the design of the space behind the stove, Darryl added vintage corrugated tin from floor to ceiling.

← When Annie's mother traded
in her home along the sunny
beaches of Florida for a Tennessee farmhouse, she brought
along one of her favorite picks.
The stately nineteenth-century
European hutch, or cupboard,
would have been found in
a kitchen and used for the
storage of dishes and other
tableware. The configuration
of the top four drawers was
purposely designed to hold the
service pieces: cutlery, cream-
ers, salt cellars, and the like,
including candles. The lower
drawers of the same size held
table linens. While the hutch
exhibits a hint of fancy flair, it
is truly a country piece. For a
formal home it would have been
crafted in a far more ornate
fashion and never painted.

↖ A peek inside the cupboard
reveals a display of antique
plates featuring wildlife motifs
such as pheasants and ducks,
indicative of Tennessee,
mingling with a collection of
ironstone covered tureens and
serving bowls.

↑ When your oven is a showstopper brass-bedecked Hallman range, you should build your entire cook space around it. That's exactly what Darryl did for Annie, who inherited the Italian beauty from her mother and designed her own kitchen with Diane and her love of cooking in mind. But memories of dad are in the kitchen, too. Most mornings, Annie makes breakfast using his well-seasoned cast-iron skillet. As with many southern cooks, he used it for making cornbread as a side for his famous Brunswick stew.

→ On the counter, antique breadboards and vintage wooden utensils (also inherited from Diane) stand at the ready in a blue-banded ceramic pitcher. Above the range hangs a collection of antique copper cooking pots assembled over years of picking at local flea markets and antique shops. They may be pretty, but Annie puts them to use when preparing family meals.

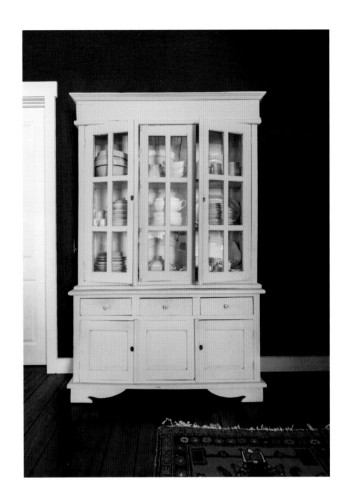

↑ Before Annie and Darryl built their cabin in the Leiper's Fork community of Franklin, they lived one town south in an old farmhouse in Spring Hill. The granddaughter of the original owner of the house gifted the egg basket to Annie. The story goes that it was used to gather eggs from the henhouse out back and the kind relative thought it should remain with Annie. When the couple moved, she took the basket along as a keepsake. Although it's lost a few splints over the years, it hasn't lost its utilitarian purpose and is still used for gathering eggs from Annie's henhouse.

↗ Farmhouse enthusiasts dream of finding a vintage cupboard like this one—a simple, stylized piece large enough to store a huge ironstone collection. All it needed to spruce it up was a fresh coat of paint. Diane used her own chalk-paint recipe, created years before commercial versions became available.

→ Mixing antique and contemporary pieces, as Annie does with her ironstone tableware, results in an eclectic, visually interesting collection (as well as a bit of history). The farmhouse hutch serves as catchall and memory keeper.

VINTAGE CRUSH

Jenni and Jared Bowlin threw their corporate jobs to the wind in favor of a more creative way to earn a living. They turned their passion for collecting antiques into a business. Now their traveling mercantile store, JBS Mercantile, offers vintage and antique picks at shows all across the country. From down-and-dirty back road barns to flea markets, thrift shops, and privately sourced pickers, the two have the demanding job of filling their trailer each and every month. Then, there's life on the road—hotel rooms, fast food, vehicle breakdowns, and nervous breakdowns too. I can

relate. Living the life of a bona fide picker isn't as romantic as it looks on TV. As daunting as the job may seem, it does have it perks—meeting up with kindred spirits along the way, new friendships that turn into family, the thrill of a great score, and the opportunity to move along a storied piece to someone who will love it as much as you do. Jenni says it fulfills her "magpie" personality and keeps her from becoming a hoarder. It's true, we can't keep it all.

When rest for the weary finally comes, no one wants to come home to a cluttered mess. Aiming to create a peaceful escape from the road, Jenni designed a space for her family with a "less is more" approach, with mindfully edited spaces that tell their story of home.

← Apothecaries are incredible pieces for storing all sorts of odds and ends or collections of small items. This 1940s apothecary still carries around traces of old pharmaceutical advertisements in its drawers. Since it's one of Jenni's favorite pieces, I don't expect it to be loaded on her trailer anytime soon. But if she changes her mind, I have first dibs.

Both Jenni and Jared are avid oddity collectors, and the couple has an admiration for things found in nature. For example, the larger than life caribou and pair of snow geese are the centerpieces of an assemblage surrounding a mercantile showcase-turned-cabinet-of-curiosities.

The nineteenth-century Victorian butterfly collection is Jenni's favorite. She approached a vendor carrying it to a booth at a show and bought it on the spot for a bargain. The encased example is a rarity; most authentic specimen collections are now conserved in museums.

↑ Jenni crafted the dreamiest kitchen by lining her open shelving with vintage and antique serviceware that is both charming and functional. The newly constructed kitchen island is designed to resemble an earlier workbench used in a craftsman's shop. Outfitted with vintage furnishings, like the schoolhouse lighting fixtures and the industrial shop chairs, it takes on a more authentic feel in keeping with the overall design of the space.

← A standout antique can be the item an entire kitchen is built around. For Jenni that was a rare form of an antique pie safe press that she found years ago at a local antique shop. The details of its past life didn't come with the piece, but it's collecting plenty of new stories at the Bowlin house.

HATS OFF

The 1800s milliner's table in the sitting room was a City Farmhouse find ten-plus years ago. Now I'm wondering how I ever let it go. A milliner's table is a furniture piece found in a millinery shop where a hatter designs, makes, trims, and sells hats.

Later in life, it wound up in a mercantile store established in the late 1800s in the tiny town of Gadsden, Tennessee. The store was well known for its large selection of wallpaper and was a major supplier of wallcoverings for all of West Tennessee. It met its demise some one hundred years later when

a tree fell during a storm and crushed the building. My picker friends Kitty and Tony were first on the scene to salvage both table and rolls of vintage paper. It was nothing that a little cleanup wouldn't fix. These old pieces are resilient, which is another reason why we want them in our homes.

ONCE UPON A TIME

When Carina Gustavsson left her home in Sweden to be an au pair for a family who were residents at the ritzy Four Seasons Hotel Atlanta, little did she know she'd be smitten by a young valet shortly after she arrived. Soon the two were sharing dreams and making lifelong plans. Now if this is all beginning to sound like a fairy tale, then hang on to your pumpkin. While it's no Cinderella story, it is a tale of finding the love of your life who somehow winds up being your business partner.

Was it luck from all those dropped pennies that Doug Jenkins picked up alongside the valet stand or just being in the right place at the right time? Either way the couple's life took another extraordinary turn not long after they met—all from a chance encounter with a businessman who frequented the hotel. The kind traveler became both friend and mentor to Carina. When she shared dreams of traveling home to see her family and somehow making a business out of it, the friendly gentleman introduced her to an antiques importer and colleague. Soon a partnership sparked among the three and Doug and Carina found themselves importing French antiques to the States to sell at shows all across the country. After eight successful years the now "married with children" couple was itching to make a

move to Nashville and strike out on their own as importers. Picking in Sweden, Denmark, Holland, Italy, Belgium, and France has offered the opportunity to source one-of-a-kind antiques for their clients and to curate a sophisticated collection for their own home.

→ Walk through the door of the Jenkins home and you'll find yourself standing in a tiny library. Interior design books, many written in Swedish, line the walls and are meticulously stacked on and beneath an antique bench. It's an interesting way to carve out a nook when space is limited. The chairs are circa 1958 by designer Børge Mogensen (he also designed the dining room chairs) and are called the Spanish Chair. Made of solid oak and leather, they are an icon of Scandinavian design, comfortable, rare, and pricey. Train your eye to scout for these marvelous pieces. Be on alert during your travels and picking trips. You never know when you may score big!

Dining at this fine circa-1970s Danish table beneath the soft glow of the rare copper Langelinie plate pendant would make anyone feel like royalty. The light was designed in 1958 for the Langelinie Pavilion in Copenhagen by designer Poul Henningsen for Louis Poulsen and was inspired by the rings of water that rippled through the bay that the pavilion overlooks. The chairs, crafted as though they were modern sculptures, are of the same era and were designed by Børge Mogensen, a Danish furniture designer who was recognized among his peers as one of the most influential designers of his time.

Leave it to a nineteenth-century trade sign to steal our hearts, especially one of this scale and design. Its black ground and gold-leaf hand lettering is still exquisite today. I love how the old light that once lit up the sign is still attached. The rare eighteenth-century Swedish burl bowl collection was gathered over many picks in Sweden. Although the couple offers a nice selection in their booths at antique shows, they save prized picks for themselves. The oldest example is dated 1676 and, as with all of them, was used in Swedish kitchens for the preparation and storage of food. Imagine the stories overheard in 300-plus years of gathering around the table. Due to their expendable nature and popularity among collectors, the bowls are getting hard to find. The size, age, and scarcity of the design of the burl determines cost.

← It's hard not to be impressed by those who have a fondness for gathering favorite little finds and then displaying the collection as if in a mini museum. For these storytellers the collected stash is proudly displayed in grandiose cabinetry oftentimes worth far more than the collections they hold. Doug and Carina accumulated these curiosities throughout their years of travel, and they overtake the space of a ten-foot antique mercantile cabinet. My favorite is the old Swedish Bible collection that fills the entire bottom shelf.

It was just before walking out the back door of the Jenkinses' house that I spied an interesting piece of art peering from behind the doorway—a vernacular watercolor of a horse, executed on paper. Intrigued, I leaned to get a closer look at the artist's name: Elina 4/27/17. Here, surrounded by rare forms of mid-century furniture, 400-year-old bowls, century-old Bibles, and exquisite examples of art, I almost missed a favorite painting. Leslie, the photographer, had already packed away her camera and we were hoping to make our way out of Nashville before rush hour, but I couldn't leave without having a photograph of this magnificent work—a humble, unframed masterpiece Scotch-taped to the wall. In case you are curious who the famous artist is, it's Elina Jenkins, Doug and Carina's daughter.

Elina 4/27/17

BOLDLY STATED

Her laughter and smile are larger than life. It's only fitting that her home is too. Celeste Shaw-Coulston's Spokane, Washington, home traces the story of the places she's traveled and her fondest memories of growing up on a farm in eastern Montana. For Celeste the dramatic black walls showcase her love for the past with meaningful decor and layers of memories filling each room. It's a uniquely styled space that is sure to inspire you to color outside the lines.

Celeste is the co-editor of *Where Women Cook Holiday* magazine and the founder of Chaps, a restaurant that she opened in a 1912 farmhouse in Spokane that evolved from cherished childhood memories of cooking alongside her Norwegian grandmother, Selma. Juggling life at the helm of these two brands is oftentimes challenging, and the stories that she comes home to comfort her and calm her mind.

At the age of eighteen a determined young woman left behind the only life she had ever known and headed west to begin a new journey in Washington state. She had lived a sheltered and secure life back in Montana and now she found herself clinging to the breathtaking landscape of her new home for comfort. She was instinctively drawn to its natural beauty and in her soul she felt as though the mountains were calling her name. Soon Celeste began gathering up vintage paintings that portrayed her new surroundings and spoke to her heart. The renderings along the foyer wall welcome her home each day just as the mountains once welcomed her to Spokane.

→ Antique front doors salvaged from cross-country trips add charm and character to the Coulston home. Each tells a story of special places Celeste and Daniel have visited.

If you aren't an old-fashioned china-cabinet kind of girl, here's a way to stow your serving pieces in something, say . . . a little more stylish. Over the years Celeste had collected a room full of mismatched china, platters, and other tableware, but finding a vintage piece with enough space to store it all together was tricky. That's when her junker extraordinaire friend Lisa offered up the large bank of lockers for Celeste to tidy up her stash. How lucky was she to find them in original white paint?

→ Common salt cellars can put on an uncommonly gorgeous show. These glass containers used for holding salt at the table were usually placed alongside each plate. With the arrival of the Industrial Revolution in the late eighteenth to early nineteenth centuries, pressed-glass manufacturers churned out the little gems in factories all across America. Easy to mold and inexpensive to make, they became one of the earliest items to be mass-produced. They also launched Celeste's collecting obsession. Her husband, Dan, gifted her a tiny glass cellar to hold her wedding ring until the day they were married. The romantic gesture inspired her to add to her collection each time the couple travels together.

← A simple object like this old-school teaching card can often stir up memories. For Celeste, it reminded her of dry eastern Montana summers when it was nearly impossible for her family to grow plants and flowers around their farmstead. She and her sisters would save buckets of rainwater in an effort to keep even the tiniest plantings alive, a sure lesson in perseverance. In the moment when Celeste found the vintage framed flashcard, memories of those hard, sweet times turned a plain object into a priceless treasure. It now hangs over an antique bench picked from a Round Top, Texas, field.

← Snoop around in most any period farmhouse and you'll discover a window over the kitchen sink. Back then it was the lookout post, where momma checked on the kids, watched for a storm to roll in, or looked for daddy to come in from the fields. But as with most modern kitchens today, Celeste's doesn't have this classic arrangement. Her authentic farmhouse sink sits mid-room, so to mimic the look she suspended an old church window above it. While she may not peer out over green pastures, the view to her family room filled with childhood mementos offers a nostalgic glimpse of home.

An antique glass-paned dish cupboard holds toy Breyer horses and cows, not just for display but also for a sentimental journey back home. The collectible toys weren't usually meant to be played with, and growing up Celeste and her sisters felt privileged when they were allowed to pull them around in their little red wagon. When her grandmother passed away Celeste made the trip back to the now-abandoned farmhouse to gather some of the items that she wanted to save. The anticipation of the trip was difficult but a friend gifted her a pair of perfectly sized ruby-red slippers. "Go home, Celeste" were the words whispered by the friend. The kind gesture consoled her, giving her the strength to go home one last time. On nostalgic days Celeste opens the cupboard to soothe her yearning for home.

CHAPTER 3

SHORT STORIES

SHORT STORIES

IDEAS TO INSPIRE CREATIVITY AND DESIGN

The furniture and accessories that we bring into our homes can be so much more than pretty decorations. They can serve us in practical ways, too. In today's world we are encouraged to practice a sustainable lifestyle, and there's no time like the present to reinvent all sorts of things for everyday use. I've learned through designing my own home that a finished space is never really finished; it's constantly evolving. It is my hope that the collections curated within this chapter will inspire you to create, and recreate, stories that instill memorable moments in both your life and home.

PUPPY DOG TALES

Many moons ago this spotted pointer stood in front of a dog kennel establishment to greet patrons looking for room and board for their pets. The large scale, the genuine collar, and the make-do repair on his tail made him so doggone cute I just had to bring him home.

Today this former trade sign takes the stage on an 1800s apothecary. When styling a substantial piece of furniture, consider using a single large objet d'art instead of a collection of smaller decorations. The life-size scale of the trade sign together with the large proportion of the antique apothecary make a bold and striking statement.

A NEW STORY FOR COLLECTED PIECES

It's always exciting to reimagine something—to bring new life to old pieces or to find a unique purpose for something that has been tossed aside. It's creatively empowering and comes with a big dose of "feel good" and pride. Plus, when the cost is minimal, that's something to write home about, as the old saying goes. Many things that you already have at your fingertips can be repurposed in a rewarding and satisfying way. And from what experts say, we have a lot on hand; it seems that only one percent of the stuff we buy is still in use even six months later (although I venture to say that we who genuinely love antiques and vintage weren't included in that survey. Toss something out? Never!). Here are seven repurposing ideas that will encourage you to begin designing and enjoying things in your home with a more purpose-driven spirit.

REIMAGINING PRODUCE TABLES AND PALLETS

A primitive produce table makes my heart go pitter-patter. I see it more as a piece of sculpture than a roadside stand. My secret dream is to own an art gallery just so I can place this castaway in a context far removed from its origins. Till then I'm putting it to use as a potting table for my most-loved winter flower, the paperwhite. Once the bulbs are planted in containers for sprouting I scatter them in sunny spots throughout the house. This year, though, I'm using this fantastic shelf repurposed from a discarded shipping pallet to create a living still life while the bulbs come into bloom. After it's served its purpose I'll restyle the table and pallet with vintage books and treasures I can enjoy all year long.

Shelves made from a reclaimed shipping pallet may be just the ticket for a bare wall in your home. These functional, decorative, and easy DIY projects can spruce up any room. They require only a few modifications and minimal materials, and they can be completed in a weekend. If you know someone who has an old throwaway pallet, this project is practically free to make. You can find tutorials for making this clever pallet shelf on many online DIY sites by searching "DIY pallet shelf."

MORE THAN A PRETTY BASKET OF FLOWERS!

This handmade French basket has been one of my most-loved finds, yet it was left to take up space on a shelf in the garage. How could I let something so beautiful sit idly by and collect nothing but dust? Its large size limited the design options, that is until I was inspired to put it on display as a farmer's market basket on my kitchen table. Its abundant size and shallow walls are both handy and stylish for gathering the harvest. It is one of my go-to farmhouse staples.

↑ All that stands between you and a great picnic is a charming basket. Begin by lining the basket with a checkered tablecloth; it will come in handy for spreading on the grass.

Wrap sandwiches in waxed paper tied with twine or string. Hand-rolled paper cones make excellent potato chip holders. Tuck in a rosemary plant for a fragrant centerpiece.

TO HAVE
AND TO HOLD

We story collectors often struggle with that great deal that we just couldn't pass up, or with family hand-me-downs even though we have no idea how we will use them. I once had a garage full of these so-called fabulous finds. But when I decided to "use it or lose it," I discovered some favorites (the trio pictured at right) that actually serve a functional purpose.

David built a stand to honor the Amish apple-picking basket (a throwback to the time it cradled fruit plucked from the tree).

The ironstone water basin—now a berry bowl—brought back memories of tagalong trips with my grandfather to the local barber shop.

When my mother was a teenager she worked behind the candy counter at the local Woolworth's five-and-dime. She weighed out hundreds of pounds of candy on this well-worn scale that now holds confections or fruit in my kitchen.

IT'S NOT WHAT THE FRENCH WOULD DO . . .

Charcuterie (a French term for the preparing of meats), thoughtfully arranged with cheeses, fruits, nuts, and home-made breads on an antique breadboard, has been a chic trend for a while. One Christmas Eve the smorgasbord of char-cuterie staples was prepped when I discovered that I had sold all of my antique bread-boards. So I reached for the French mattress smoothers that hung on my kitchen wall, although they were never meant to display food (their purpose was to fluff and smooth feather-ticking mat-tresses). What started as a fluke is now a tradition. I wouldn't think of using anything else.

GLASS ACT

We can thank, or blame, the Victorians for most of the lavish tableware found in the world. Now every thrift store has its fair share of the more common pieces, which got me thinking . . . why aren't we putting all these fancy compotes, relish trays, and etched-glass bowls to use? You can usually pick up pieces for a song, or better yet, raid your grandmother's cupboard. I repurposed these preserve compotes for single-serving salads, but you can use them for making any dining occasion special.

LESSON LEARNED

Encouraging kids to learn about the past and to value things that are meaningful to you can be tricky. To pique their interest, try making it a game at the dinner table. Here (from left to right), a Native American bead, a rare nineteenth-century Swedish Christmas ornament, a silver salt spoon and strawberry fork, a cookie cutter shaped like a Bible-toting Mennonite preacher, and an antique French ladies' pocket watch get the conversation started at our table. I simply rolled up a dinner napkin for each child and attached the interesting charm to it. To put it in play the children pass around each object and weigh in on what it could be and how it is used.

CREATE COLORFUL NAPKINS

It's easy to transform basic napkins to make any table special. A bundle of flour-sack dish towels and a couple of packets of fabric dye is all you need for this entertaining project with the kids.

EASY AS PIE

Is there anything that says summer more than peach cobbler fresh from the oven? At dusk we head to the porch with overflowing pie plates in hand to watch the lightning bugs, listen to the katydids, and fill our bellies. This was my grandmother's favorite summer pastime and I've enjoyed passing the tradition on. The standard serving method is in a bowl, but I got creative and used a vintage pie pan.

Today the embossed tin pie pans are more collectible than useful. Back when mommas and grandmas baked fresh pies for supper, every kitchen had two or three.

Perhaps it was the memory of Momma's pies brought straight from the oven that gave me the idea to repurpose them as serving dishes for cobbler. A great alternative maybe, but one small problem—they are perforated. For an easy fix, I simply lined them with waxed paper. The little clay balls in the dome are pie crust weights and when they're not in use, I use them as decoration.

TRADING PLACES

SHOP YOUR HOME FOR A FIVE-MINUTE MAKEOVER

I'm proud of the stories that are told throughout our home. The furnishings that make up these spaces were handpicked with intention, and it brings me joy to see family and guests connect with us through these visual narratives. Sometimes the story gets a bit old though. Not in the sense that I'm ready for it to go away, but simply that I have grown tired of seeing it in the same spot all these years (or sometimes, I admit, just a matter of months). It's not necessary to buy something new or make over an entire room to satisfy this yearning for change. Simply refreshing a wall or moving the furniture to a new spot will usually do the trick. Put yourself in the mindset that you are at a gorgeous antique show or flea market (depending on your picking style) and shop away. Each of these inspiring makeovers is quick, simple, arranged with furnishings on hand, or exchanged with decor from another room. Shop your own stuff! You are only five minutes away from a fabulous new look.

CHANGE
OF SPACE

↖ Doug and Carina Jenkins (page 108) live in a small home with limited space that prohibits the swapping out of larger pieces, yet that didn't stop them from restyling the walls and surfaces of furniture that had to stay put. The circa-1880s chest of drawers from France welcomes guests just inside the doorway, and a circa-1960 Danish abstract painting hangs as a colorful complement to the dark chest below. Often the chest's surface is adorned with a vintage studio lamp and a carved Swedish wooden horse, but when even the most cherished treasures begin to feel a bit mundane it's a signal that it's time for a change.

↑ Although the space didn't allow for a new furniture arrangement, Doug shifted the chest of drawers and the peasant's chair slightly off-center to give the space a fresh vibe. A 1960s abstract Mondrian painting from an art school was borrowed from the dining room to effect an element of change. While the studio lamp stayed behind, the carved figure of a horse was replaced with a signed bronze bust found on a trip to Finland.

BOLDLY
STATED

↖ Domino-colored walls bring as much drama to this space as the artwork that hangs on it. Afraid to go bold with black? It's actually a neutral color and is a backdrop that gets along well with most periods and styles, which makes redesign a breeze. Remember there's more than one shade on the color wheel, so test the waters with at least four color swatches before you dive in. Begin with painting an accent wall; often it's all you need.

Although sparsely furnished, this room feels cozy thanks to the wall color and the charming tourist portraits painted in 1942 along Chicago's Edgewater Beach. They create a graphic display, accenting the nineteenth-century Pennsylvania pottery jar that sits alongside two fine French confit pots of the same period. When designing a minimalist space choose quality over quantity. Select objects that are statement pieces, larger in scale, and artfully crafted.

→ With a black wall as your canvas it's simple to change the style and mood of a room, and to allow your collections to take center stage. While the portraits and pottery vessels offer a nostalgic vibe, a vintage abstract painting by Tennessee artist Robert Witherspoon, along with an antique Cherokee basket—both important works—create a more sophisticated atmosphere.

TWICE AS NICE

↖ One of my all-time most versatile furniture scores is this antique medical cabinet. Once used in a doctor's office, it has a sturdy steel construction and porcelain tabletop that lends itself to many decorating ideas. It's been a TV stand, a nightstand, a valet in the bathroom, and a pretty entryway piece (as shown here). An antique blackboard salvaged from a church in Pennsylvania hangs as a minimalist work of art above it. The vintage chains that securely suspend it from the ceiling become part of the art installation.

↑ Around the holidays the medical cabinet gets a refresh as a mini wine bar. It's the perfect size for a small party. I switched the blackboard for an antique road sign that David had hanging over his worktable in the garage (nothing is off limits when I'm on a mission). *STOP* is the perfect sentiment to encourage leaving work behind to relax.

↓ When a favorite piece offers both style and function, I consider that a delightful bonus. The top drawer of the cabinet is a smart storage solution for stowing napkins and bar tools. The cabinet doors beneath are handy for extra bottles of wine and serving pieces when needed.

ARTFUL MOVES

↑ Simply changing the location of a painting can change a room's look. Scoring a portrait of a dog is pretty rare, so I consider Rover to be a permanent story in the house. He's been moved about so much he feels like a rescue, but each new home gives me the feeling that he was recently adopted. He had hung out over a primitive table for a while so I thought a change would do us both good.

↑ Tight spaces offer interesting opportunities. In my home I wanted to refresh a wall that didn't lend itself to a lot of styling options. It's immediately inside a doorway, meaning floor space is just as scarce, and most furniture pieces are unadaptable. I rummaged through the house as if I were scouring a barn, and came away with this antique easel. It has the feel of a furniture piece but with a light and airy design in keeping with the scale of the space. The vintage studio chair didn't come with the easel but it offers perfect seating for an artist at work. It's wonderful when things that seem to be meant for each other finally connect to tell a new story.

SIMPLY
SAID

↖ Often a singular, meaningful object is all you need to make a statement in a room. When Laura and Daniel (page 89) left Florida, they brought along the timeworn sign that had hung from the barn on their property. It was so aged and weathered that the former trade name painted on the whitewashed board had vanished, and that's what Laura loved about it. She brought it into the dining room of her new home in Tennessee and highlighted it on a console table.

↑ With the approach of Thanksgiving Laura retires the sign through the Christmas season to make room for the hand-carved folk-art snow goose. The articulated neck of the goose folds to mimic a sleeping hen. The form is stylized and minimal—a showpiece on the marble-top console. It acts as a silhouette against the crisp white wall; no additional adornment is needed.

THE ART OF A STORIED DISPLAY

Telling your story with vintage collections brought into your home can seem overwhelming. You fall in love with the pieces but don't exactly know what to do with them. Through my business, City Farmhouse, I am exposed to a lot of spectacular finds. More often than not, if I'm drawn to something, I tend to buy it, thinking I'll figure out what to do with it later. My own home is eclectic, a style of decorating that is accepting of unexpected objects being brought into the space. Yet traditional home designers may feel that approach isn't staying true to their style.

Here's how to set your mind at ease: Treat the piece as art. Introducing a fresh oddity into your home is a great way to experiment. All it takes is a little patience and a bit of playing around to find the perfect spot. And at the end of the day, if it doesn't feel right, remove it. If it's a little quirky for the space but you still love it, then leave it. Your home shouldn't be about design rules. It should be about decorating with intention—the intention to surround yourself with the things that make you, and your family, happy. I hope you'll find inspiration in these curated vignettes from my own home, and that they will encourage you to design a space you love coming home to.

→ A simple miniature antique silhouette becomes a focal piece and creates visual interest along with the straight lines of an original nineteenth-century primitive blanket box. The simple composition acts as a work of art for the space.

BARN REVIVAL

In nineteenth-century Upstate New York, a livestock barn was raised on land that was part of a hundred-acre farm. The large hayloft stored food for the animals throughout the seasons. Built to withstand the test of time, the hayloft floor was solid, slatted for venting, and constructed of oak. Yet more than a century later the barn had long stopped serving its purpose, and with no one to manage its upkeep it had given way to the harsh elements and collapsed.

Thanks to keepers of the past these fallen barns are now salvaged and given new life through home and farm construction and restoration, crafted into furnishings, and, when no longer functional, reimagined as art. When the dilapidated barn fell it altered the loft floor's slatted rungs and severed bits of its mortised construction. Although no longer safe for a hayloft, its journey had fashioned it into a stunning wall decoration. In keeping with its natural wood and patina, I paired it with an antique side table in complementary neutral tones and hung a vintage utilitarian light, lowered to become a part of the installation. A large antique French storage jar holds natural maiden grass cut from the field.

← The primitive cupboard seemed the perfect catch-all for a young wave rider. It holds a tattered flag, a selection of ink wells and bottles, mail (love letters, perhaps), a collection of California beach shells, and daily newspapers. A torn scrap from the paper tacked inside the door provides the local weather and tide reports, forecasting the ideal time to catch a wave or two.

SURF'S UP

Laguna Beach, a small coastal town in Orange County, California, is known for its gorgeous shoreline that borders seven miles of hidden coves and majestic canyons. A noted artists' colony, painters, photographers, and filmmakers began arriving as early as 1920. But the artists aren't the only ones who have discovered their passion here. The town also has a rich surfing history centered on a five-block stretch of rocky reefs between Brooks and St. Ann's streets. During a four-month window in summer, the town swells with professionals and amateurs alike looking to catch a wave. The many resident artists line the beaches and boardwalk hoping to paint a portrait of a surfer who would take their work home or attract the attention of a tourist looking for a souvenir.

Laguna Surfer, a mixed-media work of watercolor and pencil, was painted in 1981. I hung the rendering of the attractive young surfer over a worktable and created a beach hut theme around it, incorporating a faded pale-blue storage cabinet styled with vintage soda bottles and casual surfer gear.

HANG IT UP— VINTAGE CLOTHING STYLE

I was a late bloomer when it came to discovering a love for vintage clothing. Never known as a fashionista, I hadn't noticed that it had surpassed the hippie-chic and musician crowd to line the closets of young professionals, runway models, and Hollywood's own. Which got me to thinking—who wore these threads before they hit the thrift store racks?

It was the Levi's orange-tab, Big E denim jeans I had purchased at an estate sale fifteen years ago, then packed away in a closet, that prompted me to take a second look. It wasn't long before rifling through racks at New York City thrift stores became a passion, and on more than one occasion I had to purchase a cheap suitcase or two to get it all home.

It seemed that a lovely curated vintage wardrobe shouldn't be hiding in a closet. So I crafted a plan to design a personal valet along a bedroom wall. A nineteenth-century pegboard used for corralling jackets and a collection of vintage coat hangers was just right for hanging select pieces I wanted to admire when I wasn't wearing them. The clothes were interesting enough on their own, but including cool vintage collections like the California state flag and rummage sale sign took the display to another level. This old-school approach to hanging garments doubles as an eye-catching storage solution when closet space is limited.

A chance encounter at an antique show in Texas led me to a New York dealer in the know, who introduced me to a clothing watch list. For five glorious days he took me under his wing, giving me a crash course in the art of collecting and acquiring vintage clothing. This gorgeous 1940s moleskin *bleu de travail* French worker jacket (opposite, far right) is a coveted find for collectors and vintage style seekers alike. The name translates as "working blues," for the simple chore jacket worn by French laborers.

The former shop cabinet turned jewelry chest complements the collection and serves as a functional accessory. The pink vintage model camper on top was a gift from my friend Gina—I finally found a cool spot to show it off.

TIPS FOR PICKING VINTAGE SWAG

If, like me, you are late to the party but want to add a little vintage swag to your wardrobe, here are a few tips I picked up from a pro in the know.

1. Denim is hot, particularity Levi's and Wrangler jackets. The most desirable are those made in the U.S.A. If you find a "true vintage" model, meaning it was sewn in the 1950s or before, you have scored a valuable piece for your wardrobe.

2. Seek out vintage men's white T-shirts (especially new, old stock). Popular for both guys and gals, they have a different feel than the contemporary versions. Vintage band T-shirts are having a moment too.

3. Dressier clothing from the 1960s and '70s is popular, particularly among young professionals.

4. Look for designer labels such as Chanel, Hermès, and Gucci.

5. Buy what you love, but develop an eye for quality.

6. When shopping for handbags and luggage, you will never go wrong with vintage Louis Vuitton or a Kate Spade (which is easier on the pocketbook).

→ Not all vintage clothing comes with a label. From the early twentieth century to the 1970s, most homemakers were quite handy with a sewing machine. This sweet summer dress was likely sewn during the 1950s: Its cherry-red color and peppy polka dots were common on printed fabrics of the era. A pretty little number for date night, and a first kiss at the door.

↗ The value of a vintage denim jacket is determined by its condition. Usually, a perfect one is almost impossible to find, since they were work jackets. While many collectors would prefer the pristine, there are those who seek the "thrashed." These garments show excessive wear, fraying, and patches. The authentic repairs and multiple patches on this 1960s Wrangler Blue Bell (Cliff Booth) make it highly desirable. The 1960s Wrangler Western shirt in patriotic colors is of the same period.

IS IT REALLY VINTAGE?

Knowing if a garment is truly vintage takes hands-on practice. For beginners, here are a few tips for examining tags and labels that will give you a head start.

1. "One size fits all" was a popular tag used in the 1980s.

2. Garments produced before 1980 have a lot, or style number, on the tag below the label, or sometimes this tag is found along the seam within the body of the garment.

3. The quality of a vintage label is different from those found on contemporary clothing. It has an upscale look and feel and oftentimes an unusual font style.

4. Some garments will come bearing tags with the identification of the International Ladies' Garment Workers' Union (called a Union label).

If the tag is red, white, and blue, the garment was sewn between 1974 and 1995.

5. Look for tags that identify the garment as being made in the U.S.A. In the mid-1980s, clothing was made in the Philippines, Korea, and Hong Kong. If it was made in China, India, Thailand, Bangladesh, Vietnam, Indonesia, Guatemala, Mexico, or Sri Lanka, it is not vintage—unless you consider the '90s vintage, which some do today.

→ Antique vintage ledgers run the gamut from mercantile stores to factories; even banks kept their business transactions on the ruled pages of these bound books. Every now and then I run across an interesting trade name that piques my interest—like the Wabash Screen Door Company's records from 1952. So many childhood summer memories tie into the sound of a screen door opening and slamming shut that I bought the ledger for sentimental reasons.

THE LINE ON LEDGERS

Ever wonder what something cost way back when—the salary for a week's work, or the trading stats of a stock or commodity on the New York Stock Exchange? Study an antique ledger or trading chart and you'll discover quite the financial tale. Before computerized spreadsheets and QuickBooks, the means by which a merchant or business documented their profit and loss was by hand in large, cumbersome ledgers. Highs and lows of commodities and stocks traded on the New York Stock Exchange or Cotton Exchange were inked out in printed graphs and charts.

Today these financial records from days long past are sought after for interior design applications in homes and offices. If you're on the lookout for unique pieces to style a coffee table, desk, or bookcase, ledgers are quite common, making them easy to find at most antique shops and shows. You may even get lucky and score a stack at a flea market. Earlier volumes are often leather-bound but sometimes pricey. Charts and graphs, on the other hand, are scarcer. Here, an early example factors the trading of weekly highs, lows, and futures for wool tops (the semi-processed fibers from raw wool, ready for spinning) on the New York Cotton Exchange. Salvaged from a defunct mill in Ohio, the vintage tally sheet is perfect for decorating an office space.

MY BABY, SHE WROTE ME A LETTER

I have a soft spot for the art of letter writing. Long after the sentiments are penned, delivered, and read, letters remain as tangible memories of our lives. So when I find these stories, I bring them home for safekeeping. If you are a hopeless romantic, or looking for a sentimental journey, get your hands on a stack of letters. Through reading these folded, sometimes crumpled, pages, I too have fallen in love with the handsome soldier who wrote his lovely bride nearly every day from across the miles. I've laughed at breakups, makeups, and a gal named Ruth who asked her suitor to bring along a pair of silk stockings each time he came to call. I've oohed over the birth of a newborn baby, cried when grandma died, and was shaken over a deliberate lie told more than a century ago. The next time you run across a box lot at an auction or flea market, take these memories home to honor and preserve this long-standing tradition.

In 1929 mail delivery throughout the country (and even within the same city) could take weeks. When a person—say, a certain brokenhearted suitor—needed to send a message expeditiously, that required a telegram through Western Union. The message was transmitted by Morse code over a wire then hand-delivered by a courier. Such was the urgent need of Jim to reach Miss Glenn Johnson in the summer of 1929 in the framed telegram shown here.

Dear Glenn, Needless to say that I am sadly disappointed in you. Had planned to be with you today but after you doing as you have think it useless. Will say that I have enjoyed being with you so much and regret that you do not care as much as I had anticipated. Why did you hang up while we were talking? Don't think you will have opportunity any more. With love and best wishes always. Your disappointed Jim.

to confess

CREATE A
STILL LIFE FROM
VINTAGE FINDS

Soft shades of gray and white give this space—designed to mimic a still life—a welcoming vibe. The antique French hanging apothecary that once held buttons in a French sewing room is an eye-catching display in its own right. A worn painter's canvas prepped in gray offers no clues to the intended masterpiece, yet the passage of time has contributed a warm patina to its surface that now resembles an artful abstract. Vintage mercantile signage stands offer serendipitous moments captured through forgotten photographs.

Nostalgic moods expressed through thoughtful design can contribute to a restful space. To achieve this look, assemble collections of similar tone and texture, then add interest by creating a personal moment, as I did by including the snapshots pulled from my photography collection. Make your still life special to you by displaying photos of family members.

WILD CARD

If you've read this far you are likely noticing a pattern—I look at objects with an eye to how they can be displayed as art. When you view the world outside of traditional practices, you open your mind to new and exciting possibilities.

These nineteenth-century cabinet cards, although interesting, are fairly common. I studied the images, searching for an idea that would transform them into more exaggerated works of art. If you aren't familiar with altered art, it is the concept of altering everyday objects to become decorative pieces using a variety of techniques and materials. It's a form of recycling—a way to give these mundane pieces a vibrant new life.

My goal was to adorn the subjects of the old black-and-white photos with whimsical attire painted on in bright colors, but I wasn't sure how to accomplish it. So I invited my artist friend Erin over for an afternoon of wine sipping and creative brainstorming. Soon the Victorian ladies and nicely dressed gents were wearing fresh outfits that would have been entirely inappropriate for the period. The outrageous costumes made us giggle like schoolgirls, so we decided to invite the kids to join us. I loved that it exposed them to art in an imaginative way. To try it with your own family, simply bundle up a stack of cabinet cards, invest in a few sets of paint pens, and let the creativity begin. It's a great way to eliminate boredom on those cold, rainy days when you're stuck in the house.

THE ART OF THE MAKE-DO SEAT

The most undervalued, least-sought-after antique in the twenty-first century is the country ladder-back chair. What in seventeenth-century Colonial America was a typical household furnishing has now, for the most part, been kicked to the curb. Comfort, or lack thereof, is usually the reason. By the eighteenth and nineteenth centuries fashionable furniture makers were adding elaborate refinements and greater scale to seating, making the lowly country chair less desirable. Until the late twentieth century they remained commonplace in country homes, but more for aesthetic reasons than for actual use.

Many of the earlier examples have lost their original woven rush seats and any materials that happened to be on hand were used as alternatives to repair them. It is for this reason that I cherish these make-do's and bring them into my home as folk art. This primitive replacement consists of woven strips of tin cut to resemble the original caning. While it's not the most comfortable seat in the house, it still functions well today and tells the story of a simple time when a resourceful craftsman preserved a furniture piece in a most unusual way—not for style but from necessity.

KITCHEN CLOSED
EXCEPT ON WEEKENDS

Introducing character and a whole lot of charm to a kitchen hallway is a vintage sign that once served as a notice of holiday closures in a post office. There is a brass plate for each red-letter day (which can take the place of the permanently affixed Election Day observance) along with weekday shutdown options offering plenty of reprieves from kitchen duty—although it looks like you'll have to work weekends. Beneath the sign an antique cast-iron mailbox (from a hotel lobby in New York) becomes a noteworthy catchall for mail and an ideal fit for the long, narrow space.

Since this walking space between foyer and kitchen is seen by everyone who enters through the door, my plan was for it to be as visually interesting and stylish as the other spaces in my home. But adding anything more than wall decoration in a high-traffic hallway can be tricky, so be patient in order to find just the right piece. The narrow postal box fits snuggly against the wall without taking up too much floor space. It fit my requirement for being big on charm with the added bonus of providing storage space for my cookbooks. On special occasions like birthdays it has served as a clever way to deliver presents. And its gold leaf decoration blends nicely with the holiday closure sign.

PEN PALS

Long gone are the days of searching out pen pals from faraway places through addresses in the back pages of magazines. Today it's much more than words strung together on pretty stationery, tucked into a matching envelope, licked shut, and sent on its way with a postage stamp. Through social media we're now simply a sign-in away from finding new friends, following along as they design their spaces, and eventually connecting on a more meaningful level. I have met so many wonderful people this way. Come along for a snapshot peek behind the squares of six friends and home designers that first made their way into my life on the Instagram platform. I've now met all but two in person, and one became my very best friend.

← In keeping with a theme of decorating with objects found in nature, Becki Griffins (page 162) has gathered a fascinating collection of butterfly specimens to hang above (and to accent) a vintage farmhouse cabinet. The storage piece once hung on a wall, but in Becki's home it's better served as a console. A hummingbird's nest and a collection of leather-bound books contained in vintage cloches bring more natural texture into the space.

SENTIMENTAL STYLE

Creating a lovely home has always been a priority for Becki Griffin (@curiousdetails); she does it both professionally and personally. The Texas decorator is a prop stylist, which means she styles a homeowner's space for a magazine's editorial images. Styling for a publication is far different than decorating a home. In preparation for a shoot, the spaces are thoughtfully edited to create a clean visual for the camera's eye. At home, Becki decorates with her own style and taste and for the comfort of her family. Her collections tell the stories of who she is, her travels, and what she loves.

There was a time when Becki spent her weekends scouring estate and garage sales, thrift and antique shops, or any place she could score a piece with character for a bargain. Now her home brings the finds from all those successful hunts together.

The antique church sign is a daily visual reminder of growing up in a small town in Texas from where, she says, each and every blessing in her life has flowed. She picked it for a song at an antique shop in Houston, long before architectural antiques were in vogue. The sign has been a feature story in every house she has owned—and she would never part with it. The vintage shutter cabinet was a five-dollar garage sale find, which she spruced up by painting it black and distressing it. It gets along well with the church sign, thanks to the rehab, and provides plenty of extra storage to boot.

The framed pressed botanicals were pulled from the dollar bins at a thrift store, and although they are not rare antiques, they have the look of vintage herbariums. In the wooden bowl, smooth rocks gathered from the Frio River are a reminder of the family's time together combing the shorelines of beaches and rivers and collecting natural artifacts that they find interesting throughout their travels.

LUCKY HEARTS

My social-media-acquaintance-turned-best-friend, Ruth Barnes (@southernjunkersvintagemarket), is a gold digger, but not in the usual sense—some things are more precious than the shiny metal. Her historic home on the outskirts of Memphis sits on four acres that were once part of a larger farm. Former tenant shacks that housed laborers still dot the southern landscape today, and it is the land surrounding these dwellings where Ruth's "gold" is discovered.

Ruth has been digging into the past for years, unearthing broken crock lids, shoes, and other discards of the former tenants. The ground is especially fruitful with discarded bottles, and the dig frequently yields common clear glass in many shapes and sizes.

While any discovery brings satisfaction to a bottle digger, it's the hopes of snagging a rare specimen that keeps the thrill of the hunt alive. And that's just what happened to Ruth one blustery winter day when, overcome with cabin fever, she ventured out on a dig. The winter winds had covered the grounds with fallen leaves, with no bookmarks of the former repositories visible. Yet something—perhaps it was a bit of magic radiating from a certain bottle that led Ruth to dig beneath a tree that she had often passed over. As she pulled a bottle from the ground, a sparkling heart appeared embossed with the words *Lucky Heart*. Score! Ruth had unearthed a story—one of a secret history, of cosmetics, perfume, and hoodoo!

Lucky Heart Cosmetics, located on Mulberry Street in Memphis, was founded during the Great Depression, one of the local manufacturers of a line of cosmetics geared toward African American women. From Ruth's research, she found that Lucky Heart's early success was attributed to a little more than all that "smell good" and "look good"; it was a concoction of another story—"curios"—oils, powders, incense, and herbs used in folk healing. With that storied past now long behind them, Lucky Heart Cosmetics remains in business today and is one of the founding members of the National Civil Rights Museum.

THEY BROKE BREAD IN THEIR HOMES AND ATE
TOGETHER WITH GLAD AND SINCERE HEARTS

ACTS 2:46

TRAIL BLAZERS

For fifteen years, Jen Hamilton (@wheresisters-gather) and her husband, Dave, painstakingly restored a 1900s farmhouse that happens to be part of a unique story—it sits on a county historical site along the Oregon Trail. The couple rolled up their sleeves and tackled most of the renovation projects themselves, including the addition of a wraparound porch—a priority for seasonal kicking back. Including vintage and antique finds in their farmhouse decor—picked by Jen at flea markets and thrift stores—was their way to continue their story and bring local history into play. Being united as a couple in goal and purpose, and then seeing the fruits of their labor come to pass, has been, Jen says, a life-changing experience.

GATHER HERE

For a clever sideboard in the dining room, Jen repurposed a vintage nursery cart using barnwood slats. Filled with a thoughtfully curated collection of timeworn treasures, the accessories aren't just for show. They are called into play every day for prepping and serving meals.

Above the sideboard, a salvaged and chipped DIY frame holds a work of art stenciled and hand-painted with one of Jen's most-beloved Bible verses. The first thing that family and guests see when they enter the home, the piece is not only welcoming but also announces that togetherness is cherished here. Whether it's her family gathered around a simple meal or lingering long with neighbors and friends, sharing her home in the spirit of gracious hospitality is Jen's goal of living with purpose and intention.

↑ A vintage utility shelf is Jen's solution for decorating the odd corner between the window and wall. Filled with artfully arranged farmhouse collections, the grouping offers a pleasing aesthetic without feeling cluttered.

Jen took the cow (painting) on a stroll around the house before deciding it should hang unframed over the shelf. The Sand Pass Creek trail sign has the feeling of being plucked straight from the Oregon landscape.

SIGNS OF HOME

Seasoned pickers who shop the Springfield Antique Show/Extravaganza and Flea Market in Springfield, Ohio, know the secret for the best picking—get there before daylight on load-in day to shop "the line." Jane Peet (@gritantiques) has Ohio roots. Her dad was born and raised just a few miles down the road in Cincinnati, and it was her birthplace as well. Now living in North Carolina, Jane and husband, Shaun, thought it would be a great adventure to road trip it to her favorite stomping grounds and shop—the Extravaganza. The couple was quite familiar with the "pecking order" that often takes place at this large market. Sellers consider certain members of a group of antique aficionados who are die-hard pickers to be particularly good buyers. These pickers hit the ground running as soon as the trucks start to unload and, if lucky, they get the coveted first pick.

As the couple fearlessly shopped the line, Jane spotted a large sign in the back of a seller's truck. Not wanting to miss the opportunity to score a find for his better half, Shaun bypassed the spectators waiting for the unload and jumped right in. This type of aggressive picking behavior isn't uncommon when a prized treasure is up for grabs. He opened his wallet without hesitation, paid the seller, and walked away with the sign. Turns out it wasn't a trade sign after all; it is a salvaged fragment from an antique feed scale. For Jane it serves as a reminder of where she's from, the roads she's traveled, and the memory of her dad, who had a deep affection for his hometown.

Honor your memories as Jane did by hanging a single large piece as a focal point in a family or dining room, or combine design with sentiment by creating a gallery wall depicting meaningful milestones, celebrations, or significant places.

THE BUTTON PICKER

I met Anne Karp (@splendidjunkvintage) for the first time at a Country Living Fair in Rhinebeck, New York. Our friendship had taken root and blossomed through my admiration of the curated vintage finds she delivers weekly via her artfully articulated squares on her Instagram feed. She has a keen eye for seeking out quality and authenticity, then manipulating the camera's lens to capture the objects as if they were prized heirlooms—and sometimes they are. Her musings usually tell the story of where she's found them, often peppered with humorous anecdotes of behind-the-scenes shenanigans.

According to Anne, it wasn't her fault that she became a button collector. Rather, it was the mysterious calling of the objects that repeatedly drew her to them. It seems that Anne can sniff out a tin of buttons at a local estate sale from miles away.

Most of her early picking happened at estate sales and was limited to a couple of hours on mornings when her young boys were at pre-school. The logic behind the "button picking" is that most homes had a sewing machine and the sewing notions were usually stored in a tin. Nearby was a similar tin specifically dedicated to holding buttons. Even before opening the lid, Anne knew if it held buttons simply by judging the weight. Having opened the tin, she would quickly assess if there were mother-of-pearl buttons (her beloved choice) in the mix. If so, she would close the box, pay, and head off to get the boys. The tins held a range of buttons, some impossibly small and others large, those with carved patterns or crafted into shapes of clovers, hearts, or fish. Her most cherished are the ones that have remnants of string and fabric, those that were clearly saved from an article of clothing. Throughout her home there will always be displays of mother-of-pearls corralled in ironstone bowls, shining brilliantly in glass jars, and, yes, rattling around in old tins.

MOTHER-OF-PEARL: SPOTTING THE REAL DEAL

If you have a love for antique mother-of-pearl buttons but aren't sure how to spot a fake, here is a foolproof tip—run it across your pearly whites. It's true: Gently rub the button across the edges of your teeth. If it feels gritty, it's real. Also, mother-of-pearl buttons are made from the inside layer of freshwater and saltwater mollusk shells, which gives the button its distinctive rainbow luster. This natural shine is hard to reproduce, so if it magically appears, you're in luck. For even more confirmation, there's the temperature test. A shell button will always feel cooler to the touch, so you may want to take along a plastic button to feel the difference.

IN SEARCH
OF A COUNTRY
CUPBOARD

Isn't this the sort of discovery that puts a grin on your face? It was just the kind of period piece my friend Catherine Pierce (@farmhouse1873) was looking for to replace the slick, shiny, built-in cherry pantry that her home's previous owners had installed during a 1980s kitchen remodel. To her it looked more like a phone booth than a kitchen piece and did nothing to enhance the authentic layered and collected look she had curated in the family's nineteenth-century stone farmhouse.

Luckily for Catherine, she happens to live in a region in Pennsylvania that is especially ripe with these farmhouse pieces, and she found, and fell for, the cupboard at an antique show in Valley Forge. Her best friend, Helen, a longtime antiques collector, who she considered an expert as well as an antiquing buddy and kindred spirit, was along for the outing (Helen has since passed). The cupboard had the most extraordinary worn green and blue paint, and storage! Taped inside one of the drawers was a note that told the story of its origin—Lynwood Mason Estate, Town Farm and East Falls Road, Harrison, Maine, circa 1870. Catherine went home that day without the cupboard, but her husband, John, knowing how much she loved it, had measured to

see if it could be a fit. At first light, he was back in the truck headed to Valley Forge to bring it home. All of the picking stars had aligned, and the cupboard has become a beloved part of Catherine's home, her kitchen, and her family, as well as her memory of a perfect day with her best picking pal, Helen. Humble yet handsome, functional and unapologetically quirky, it is a piece with timeless appeal that would play as well in a modern home as it does in this old farmhouse.

→ Catherine found the authentic Tomatoes-A-Basket sign at her favorite shop, Isabella Sparrow. In its former life it hung roadside at a farm stand in Lancaster County, Pennsylvania.

CHAPTER 4

A STORY FOR
ALL SEASONS

A STORY FOR ALL SEASONS

DECORATING FOR THE SEASONS

There's no better inspiration than the dawn of a new season. Each has a special story to tell. It's not just the changing colors—from showy displays to winter white—but also the feelings that arise within us, of enthusiasm, optimism, new beginnings, and letting go. I enjoy styling my home for the seasons, but I also make it my goal to savor the moments spent with family and friends instead of fussing with elaborate displays. Here you'll discover a collection of design ideas that will inspire you to relax into the season and tell your story. By incorporating similar pieces from your own home, you can accomplish these projects in a matter of minutes—or a few hours at most. Plus, there are a few entertaining projects you can do with the kids that will give them some seasonal inspiration too.

→ A crock jar filled with pink tulips becomes the centerpiece for a nineteenth-century Swedish demilune table. An old-fashioned theater seat offers an attractive alternative to a traditional chair. The heirloom Bear Paw patterned quilt is more than a striking work of art. David and I hang it each spring as a reminder of a special memory of our honeymoon (see Story of the Bear Paw Quilt on page 179).

SPRING

The Christmas season may have inherited the phrase "the most wonderful time of the year," but for me the most wonderful season is spring—the crisp cool air, the smell of the earth, hints of green grass, budding trees, fresh green sprouts, and flowering perennials. At the first hint of spring air I'm off to the local market to gather a bouquet of tulips, daffodils, and seasonal herbs to spread throughout the house. It's the first opportunity to "bring the outside in," and the fresh blossoms are an instant way to wash away the gloom of winter.

STORY OF THE BEAR PAW QUILT

It was late afternoon on a spring day in the Smoky Mountains and David and I were enjoying a wedding day celebratory glass of champagne on our hotel balcony when we spotted a momma bear and three chubby cubs wandering out of the woods. Here we were, two floors above, and within less than 200 feet of the most adorable bear family marching straight toward us. I happen to have an endearing fondness for those charming cuddly creatures that we all want to hug yet run from at the same time. I had never seen a bear in the wild, so there was no passing up the chance to head down to get a closer look. I'm pretty certain this wasn't their first outing to the neighborhood because the triplets seemed calm and delighted to give us a little sideshow. As momma bear watched nearby, the siblings playfully wrestled each other to the ground, behaving mischievously as most kids do after being cooped up all winter. I imagined that the cubs were born in hibernation and the family was on a routine dumpster dive to the many trash receptacles that surrounded the tourist area. As I crept a bit toward them, momma gave the clue that the fun was over, and they scurried off into the woods. I jokingly told David that it was the highlight of the trip. Funny that he still makes light of it every spring when he is asked to display the quilt (page 177) on the wall.

BUNNY TALES

When springtime calls for a seasonal table display, pluck that favorite cement yard ornament from the garden, give it a good cleaning, and build an unexpected centerpiece around it. This vintage floppy-eared bunny is just what I had in mind to decorate the table for a Sunday afternoon brunch with the kids. My goal was to keep it sweet and simple, with the bunny sparsely swaddled in blooming clematis vines. The problem—it was a bit too soon for climbing flora. That meant I had to substitute with faux (never!) or call my local florist friend, Steve, to order in. Much to my surprise the florist hothouse clematis does not come as an actual vine; it is merely flower clippings. Gasp! Now my simple centerpiece project was becoming more of a frustration. To create a mock version I gathered dormant vines from outdoors, wrapped them around the bunny, then tucked the florist blooms within. In the end it turned out beautifully—it's light and airy, right for the season, and a great conversation piece.

It was never a question as to whether or not the rusty bunny basket found at the local flea market was coming home with me. Fortunately, the price tag was easy on my pocketbook, which made the score even more thrilling. Just months before, I became a grandmother, the proud "mammie" of baby girl Giuliana, and this garden basket filled with pretty springtime herbs was going to be the centerpiece in celebration of our new little family member. She had arrived in this world kicking and screaming on the most beautiful sunny day in April, and this bundle of joy just happened to be a surprise birthday present for David. It delighted him that they would forever share a bond that no one, nor time, nor distance could erase. He also knew that it meant some things would change on his special day. The homemade pineapple cake he looked forward to each year would soon be swapped for a showstopping sugary version decorated with the favorite TV character of the moment. Easter Sunday marked the day that year when Giuliana left the nursery and came home with her family, and for that reason her mom and dad nicknamed her Bunny.

← Highlight the beauty of everyday utilitarian objects by reinventing them to serve a delightful new purpose. In its former life the wooden mold was used for forming cement pavers (stepping stones). I picked it on a trip to California, and I'm drawn to its simple lines and warm wood tones. Here it is used as a pretty spring centerpiece, but it's also eye-catching as a cookie tray or a small charcuterie board. When flipped over it makes a great surface for chopping. But it doesn't limit itself to the kitchen; I once used it in the guest bathroom to hold soaps and toiletries.

WHITE DONE RIGHT

My designer friend Heather Castro has a special gift for designing classic white spaces, and she recently offered that talent to her friend Casey, who lives in a stunning Tennessee farmhouse. Once the trees began to bud outside Casey's bedroom window she called Heather in for a spring refresh. The various hues of white, along with the antique textured door, gave Heather an inspiring canvas to work her magic. To create a pretty window seat, she upholstered a pair of vintage French chairs using antique sheets made from hemp and freshened up the wood by first painting it in

Miss Mustard Seed's Milk Paint in Warm Gray, then distressing it. The center table got its own coat of whitewash in Annie Sloan Chalk Paint in Old White.

To prevent an all-white space from feeling sterile, it's necessary to incorporate texture. Heather accomplished this by adding a rustic bench and an antique distressed iron bed. Carpet, white cotton drapes, and a linen duvet cover hand-sewn by Heather contribute to the cozy vibe. Large windows bring the spring sunshine in, and soon a grassy wooded lawn will play along with unexpected pops of yellow from the wild daffodils.

SUMMER

Summer is the time of year to be outdoors. As soon as school is out our family starts planning our annual trip to the beach for fun in the sun. The weather is too beautiful to spend my days restyling my space for the season, but I do want an impactful refresh with bold colors and bouquets of summer flowers. Easy-breezy is the look I'm going for throughout this season.

↑ For those who love to create gorgeous minimal spaces that also tell a unique story, here's your mantra: incorporate unexpected design elements that are both eye-catching and functional. In this dining space an antique farm table is paired with a set of mid-century Woodard garden chairs for a summer look. The nineteenth-century apothecary, pulled from the New York City office of an electrical contractor, acts as a savvy sideboard. The room feels modern and sophisticated. When strong furnishings are the hallmark of your design, a few core pieces are all that is needed to create a stunning space.

IN THE GOOD OL' SUMMERTIME

Folk-art paintings—works by an untrained hand lacking in formal art training—are powerful and speak to my soul. They are one-of-a-kind masterpieces created out of love and sometimes loss. It is both the hand and the heart that draws us in.

With the exception of summer, the little country church painted on common Masonite by Marie Brae hangs in the attic bedroom over the watercolor of the church where David and I were married (see "Once Upon a Dusty Old Attic," page 48). Come summer, though, it makes its way to the dining room, where it hangs as a single focal point for the season over a primitive mantle. We don't know why Marie painted the church, but we do know, through her naïve detail of the cross on the steeple, the stained-glass

windows, and the meadow of blooms, she was determined to paint a realistic interpretation. A single candle in a nineteenth-century bottle is all the adornment needed to complete the humble design.

↑ Three cheers for the red, white, and blue, and for making July the easiest month to bring in decor! There's nothing more attention-grabbing than the good ol' American flag. A few buckets filled with parade-waving versions of the Stars and Stripes are all you need to show your pride and decorate your home for the season. In design, minimalism fares far better than overkill. I display my flags in an antique French grain bucket but metal pails, ice cream buckets, and large crocks work well too.

→ These naïve works of art are rooted in traditions of a community or culture and weren't usually painted to be sold but instead laid to the canvas purely as self-expression and to bring joy to the beholder.

↑ The faded blue ice cream bucket has been with me since 1995. I can't tell you how many times I could have sold it. On the days I was tempted to let it go I would close my eyes and remember how beautiful it is filled with dahlias. I have a favorite flower for each season, but the cheerful, dazzling dahlia is my go-to for both summer and fall. The overflowing bucket of blooms provides a showy display for visitors at City Farmhouse. Then in late summer and early fall, when the weather turns cooler, I take the bucket home to enjoy while back-porch sitting. The salmon-pink-painted primitive bucket bench that I picked up on a trip to Ohio accents the brilliant colors of the dahlias. The sweet marker-on-paper drawing, a gift from friend and singer/songwriter Kim Carnes, hangs above it.

↑ If a piece of art speaks to you, buy it—that is, if it's within your budget. If you are truly drawn to it you'll find the perfect space for it. This colorful summer vignette that rests on top of a white vintage chest of drawers has a folky yet modern vibe and tells many stories for me. I picked it on a book-signing trip to California. The vendor had found it along the Oregon coast, but offered no additional clues as to what had inspired the artist to paint it. It reminds me of trips to the beach with the kids, and of my friend Peggy who brought back the large conch shell as a gift when she visited her daughter in the South of France. It's a simple, done-in-an-instant look that feels collected over time.

FALL

Falling leaves, pumpkin-spice candles, jewel-tone colors, cozy blankets, nuts, pots of soup, and s'mores toasted around a campfire are a few of the things I look forward to once the heat of summer gives way to the crisp air of autumn. For me, it's a settling-in season, a time to gather with family and friends, to be thankful, and to dream up exciting projects that will create lasting memories. Carry the sentiment of thinking simply and loving deeply over into designing your home and embrace the less-is-more approach.

↑ Faded sunflowers are left to dry so their seeds can be harvested and planted come springtime. Pumpkins picked from the patch join the withering flowers and are ready to be sold to passersby who want to take one home to make into a jack-o'-lantern, or a tasty pie.

← The beauty of fall decor is that it lends itself to using readily available goods like fruits, nuts, and plants that can be picked up on a grocery store run (or maybe even on your own property). Create a striking centerpiece for your dining or coffee table, island, or sideboard by filling a wooden dough bowl, utility caddy, stoneware or ironstone bowl, or any vessel you love, with fruits and nuts of the season. Here I have stocked a nineteenth-century oversized French grain scoop, along with a smaller version used for shoveling flour, with mixed nuts, green pears, and pomegranates. I repotted the store-bought plant into a handmade folk-art flowerpot. All of this in about as much time as it took to put away the groceries.

START A FAMILY TRADITION

In our home Thanksgiving is more than pretty decorations, scrumptious food, and a reprieve from the workday. For our family it's celebrated in the same spirit as the feast of the Pilgrims in 1621—as a day to give thanks for the blessings that God continues to send our way. Each year I look for creative ideas that encourage the kids to appreciate the day and all that it stands for. These activities, although intended for the children, have wound up touching the hearts of all who gather at our table. Now it's a part of our story and a family tradition that I expect will continue for generations to come.

A large roll of ruled paper from my friend Kerri inspired a fun Thanksgiving activity with the family. When it was time to serve dessert, I rolled out the paper along each side of the table and placed a vintage craft pencil next to the dessert plate, napkin, and silverware. Our grandson, Riley, walked around to each place setting and wrote "Thankful for" in marker above the ruled lines. While we were enjoying our cake or pie, each family member wrote what they were most thankful for and then read it aloud before the end-of-the-meal prayer. It has become a Thanksgiving tradition, one that the kids talk about as soon as we sit down for the turkey and trimmings. Rolls of shelf liner or kraft paper work equally well. Simply roll the paper across the entire table and the sentiments can be written beside the plates.

LEGEND OF THE JACK-O'-LANTERN

Aren't the simplest ideas usually the best? When fall rolls around, this is the first spot I run to. I remove the farmers' market totes and rain jackets from the pegs and hang these adorable jack-o'-lanterns hand-carved from gourds. I found them many years ago at a craft show in Nashville. Handmade by an Amish family in Kentucky, they reminded me of a time before Halloween became so commercialized.

When we make caramel apples with the kids I take the jack-o'-lanterns down and place a candle inside each one to set the mood for a spooky story. It's an Irish tale of Stingy Jack, a miserable old man who played tricks on everyone he met, was kicked out of heaven, and even rejected in hell for a deal he had made with the devil himself. When Jack had nowhere to go but to wander the dark netherworld between heaven and hell, the devil took pity on him and tossed him an ember from the flames to help light his way. Jack hollowed out the turnip he had in his pocket and placed the burning ember inside. That lit lantern became known as a jack-o'-lantern.

Since I was a little girl I have loved hearing my grandmother tell that story on Halloween. The Irish brought the legend and tradition of carving a pumpkin to be lit as a lantern to America, but they usually carved turnips, rutabagas, potatoes, beets, and gourds, and not for the purpose of lighting a path to a bowl full of candy. Legend has it that on All Hallows' Eve, a candle was placed in the carved vegetables in an effort to ward off evil spirits and to keep Stingy Jack away. Pumpkins became more commonly used in the mid-1800s after Washington Irving wrote of the Headless Horseman having a jack-o'-lantern for a head in *The Legend of Sleepy Hollow*.

"M'M! M'M! GOOD!"

Was it really the Campbell's tomato soup that was "*m'm! m'm! good!*," or the cute soup mug that made it so tasty? Made by the McCoy Pottery Company in the 1960s, the mug was used as a promotion for the Campbell's Soup Company. It's been rumored that the brightly colored drinking cup was a spin-off of the tomato soup can, which was made popular in paintings by pop artist Andy Warhol in 1962. That soup-filled mug was highly favored, alongside a grilled cheese sandwich, in my grandmother's kitchen. The memory inspired me to snatch up a collection for three dollars each at an antiques mall. I pull them out at the first fall chill and share a lunchtime story with the kids.

FLAVORS OF FALL

It wouldn't seem like fall without gathering around a glowing campfire to toast fluffy marshmallows, then folding that crusty, gooey goodness inside a chocolate-bar-topped graham cracker to make a s'more. Although many of us don't live where we have access to a roaring bonfire, that shouldn't stop us from enjoying the celebrated seasonal treat. We have friends who turn a fireplace or fire pit into a make-do campfire. Unfortunately, our home has neither. But determined to have the kids experience the fall tradition, I devised a plan that not only worked perfectly but also was simple to accomplish.

A candle flame is all the heat you need to toast a marshmallow. When selecting the candle be sure to choose one that is unscented and of ample size. To elevate the ambience, I pulled the old campfire warmer from the garage—I knew one day it would come in handy. It's round, made of tin, with a door that opens to expose a small lantern that would have been filled with oil, then lit by a wick. The flame would heat the underside of the top, thus keeping warm the food that was placed on it. Although the lantern has a wick that would have provided the flame, for this project I replaced it with a candle. I grabbed the strawberry caddy and gathered all the essentials for making the s'mores, including small branches from the yard, a jar of marshmallows, a bucket of graham crackers, and chocolate bars. I added a side bucket of fresh sliced strawberries (if you've never had them on a s'more, you're in for a treat). The ceramic candlelit goblin picked at a thrift store enhanced the mood.

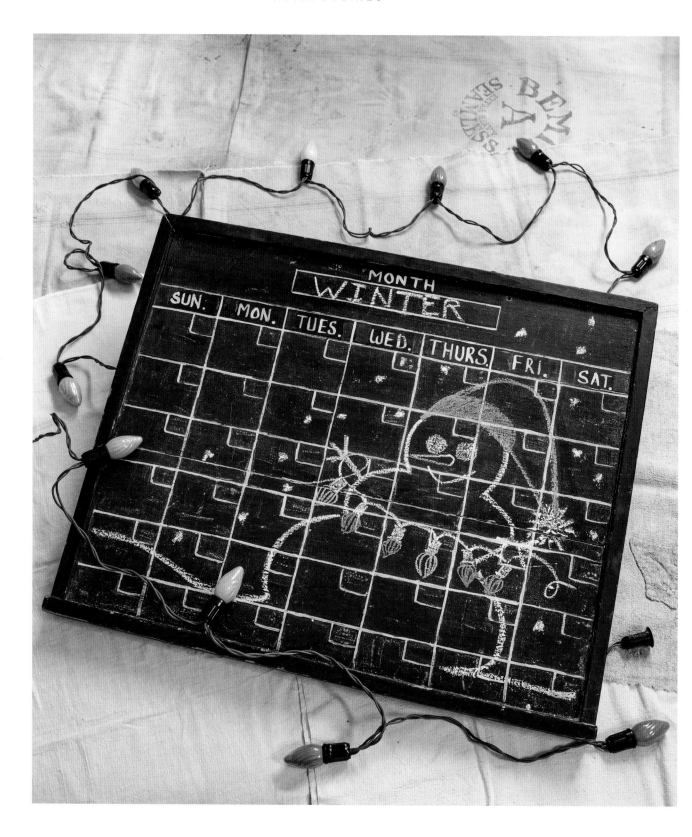

WINTER

Warm-weather lovers like me often find ourselves spending winter hibernating indoors and counting the days until the return of sunshine and pleasant temperatures. But we can ward off the winter blues by savoring these days, especially the holidays, and spending quality time with family and friends. It's the perfect season to channel your inner child, so I've included some projects that will delight kids and grown-ups alike. There are also plenty of creative yet practical design ideas and inspiration that will spark conversation in your home. After all, that's what the season is all about—connecting with those we love and the stories we share together.

GRAMMAR LESSON

If you were in English grammar class in 1826, these sweet illustrations by Willard Asaph would have appeared as you flipped through the pages of the textbook *Paths of Learning Strewed with Flowers, or English Grammar*. These examples are 1940s copies of the original color illustrations; there were twelve in all. I'm drawn to their folky character and old-world charm, and when displayed in a grouping they make for an impressive display. I hung them in the library as a winter refresh and included a nineteenth-century altar stick and stoneware bowl brimming with pinecones.

THE MAGICAL FLYING MACHINE

Perhaps there really is a Santa Claus after all. Why else would the W. N. Snow Company and the S. C. Felt Company have designed and patented such elaborate carriages if they weren't needed for magical, snowy Christmas Eve journeys and silent rooftop landings? That said, in the late nineteenth century, the jolly old elf wasn't the only one who needed a means to get about town.

The W. N. Snow Company of Snowville, New Hampshire, operated ten businesses, but it was best known for its patented spring sleighs, especially in rural areas where terrain was exceptionally rough. With a name like Snow how could the founder go wrong? Then there was the S. C. Felt Company, whose spring sleigh looks very much like Santa's flying machine. Each year it's fun to hang the patent renderings above the mantle and excite the kids with the story of how Santa's

method of travel came to be. (Except now they are too old for that, and they won't even play along for fun.) A beautifully formed silver-plate water pitcher holds holly cut from the bush just outside our door, and a felt-skinned reindeer stands at the ready to guide Santa's sleigh.

Incorporate a little magic, whimsy, and mystery into your winter styling, even if it's only to relive the childlike fantasy that lives on inside all of us.

HO-HO-HO HOT CHOCOLATE BAR

There's nothing better for drinking in the season than with hot cocoa served in a jolly old Santa mug. Back in their heyday the ceramic mugs were wildly popular and largely mass-produced, which means they aren't hard to find today. Actually, the frenzy started in the 1950s when two college students launched a Christmas gift company with a $9,000 loan from their families. The Santa mugs were so popular that the friends began creating coffee mugs for everyday use.

I loved these so much as a child that my grandmother pulled them out of the attic as soon as the Thanksgiving dinner table was cleared. Back then I thought them perfect for Christmas tea parties (the tea was really Kool-Aid). Now we use them for their intended purpose: hot chocolate. The handmade make-do cupboard is an ideal fit for holding the mugs and all the "fixin's," making it easy to whip up a hot cup on cold winter nights.

→ Our granddaughter Lila painted the sentiment "JOY" alongside a snowman as a topper for the Christmas tree. An uncommon decoration to top off a tree, but it was the gift of the hand that painted it and heart that delivered it that we proudly displayed.

GUESS AND TELL

If you are looking to step up your game this season and have a whole lot of fun with kids of all ages, then this unexpected gift-opening challenge played around the Christmas tree is for your family. Begin by wrapping your presents in white or brown kraft paper. Trim with a pretty bow (I prefer thin satin and corrugated ribbons or garden twine). Then slip a brightly colored washable marker underneath the ribbon. The object of the game is for the child or teenager to guess what's in the package and write it on the paper with the marker. The guessing game continues until they correctly figure out the prize inside or until you finally give in and let them open it. If you're a stickler for meticulously wrapped packages (or if there are delicate, breakable gifts inside), this game may not be for you. In the heat of the moment the kids often shake, rattle, and roll the gift until it looks like the dog got hold of it. If you have a dog, by the way, expect him or her to bark right along with the laughter throughout the game. You don't have to limit the merrymaking to the kids; adults love playing too. It's guaranteed to get you into the Christmas spirit.

REASON FOR
THE SEASON

A humble vintage handmade candle chandelier lights the way home and highlights the "poor man's stained-glass window" (meaning it was painted to resemble stained glass) salvaged from a church in West Tennessee. The rough-around-the-edges beauty is genuine and unpretentious. It's certainly a moving testament for the season, but its message can speak to us all year long.

Decorating for the holidays doesn't have to mean expensive store-bought decorations. Often the simplest things we've gathered over time are the most beautiful and thoughtful and the most precious to us. Envision how they can become a part of your celebration this season. Those who enter your home will be moved by your imaginative spirit and intention and will leave with a feeling of connection to the moment.

O CHRISTMAS TREE,
O CHRISTMAS TREE

A grouping of trees repurposed from nineteenth-century barn doors are just right for the farmhouse-style enthusiast who loves rustic, neutral decor. To create a majestic effect these trees were crafted in various sizes and layered standing on the floor and on a table. I picked them up at a Country Living Fair, but if you are handy with a saw, you can create your own. Here they are displayed indoors but are equally charming grouped on a porch.

CHAPTER 5

SHOPPING GUIDE

WHY BUY ANTIQUES?

1. Antique pieces come with a story that can add to your own. When antiques become a part of your home, you invite in bygone conversations and stories that can be passed on for generations to come.

2. These old-school pieces are timeless. Antiques embrace characteristics that allow them to blend well with most interiors, decor, and time periods.

3. Antiques are handcrafted and well made, built to withstand the test of time. For example, the pieces of wood used to construct furniture back in the day were joined to last. The joinery of a furniture case was usually mortise and tenon, drawers were dovetailed, and wooden pegs were often used instead of nails. If the piece is signed by the maker, that is golden. A 150-year-old table may come with a few dents and dings, but that character is the reason we love it.

4. For future returns, invest in the past—buy antiques, because they usually retain value. Ever frown when a big-box store furniture purchase gets kicked to the curb? Buying that antique piece instead may have added to your bank account should you decide sell.

SHOPPING GUIDE

When I wrote the resources chapter for *City Farmhouse Style*, I felt it was a solid guide for leading you to all the best picking spots from coast to coast. Actually, I still feel that way, but many of you reached out to me wanting to know more—like where I would shop to find a farm table or those amazing vintage doors that were featured throughout the book. Trouble was I couldn't usually answer those questions, because it wasn't my home, nor was I the one who picked it. In this book it's my house that's featured throughout. That means I'm giving you the inside scoop of where I picked most pieces, and in some instances the vendor who originally picked that beautiful piece that I brought into my home. It's all here in this comprehensive picking and shopping guide, organized by chapter and heading.

I didn't stop there. I've thrown in a few of my favorite home-goods hot spots too, plus the favorite picking holes of my "Pen Pals" (page 161) along with local picking lists from a few of the friends featured in "Other People's Stories" (page 62).

I have also included resources for escapes. If you're someone who loves an adventure and getting away with your friends for a week of fun and shopping, I suggest that you shoot an email straight away to my friend Suzie Stroup.

Not only will you find amazing pieces for your home, but you'll also be treated like a queen while you're doing it.

If you fell in love with the Sugar Shack or the Big Blue House, you'll be happy to know that you can actually stay in them. I'm sharing all the details so that you can plan your escape.

We couldn't list all the sources of course. There are many more fabulous shows, shops, malls, flea markets, thrift stores, and vendors out there that we have picked from over the years. For the purposes of this guide I have included sources for the current pieces found throughout our home and a sampling of picking spots from "Other People's Stories" and "Pen Pals." When the source is a vendor, the Instagram account is noted; a shop, mall, show, or home goods store includes contact information and location addresses.

CHAPTER 1— OUR STORY

Pages 8–9: vintage farm fragment repurposed **shelf**, Marburger Farm Antique Show, vendor @cottonseedtradingcompany; black wooly **sheep**, gift, @blacksheepfleadesigns; antique **Bible collection**, Marburger Farms Antique Show, various vendors and gifts.

Page 11: early twentieth-century New York lodge **chair**, CR-71.

First Impressions: nineteenth-century painted decorated **chest of drawers**, Heartland Antiques and Collectibles; handmade **rug** from repurposed clothing, Housing Works Thrift Shops, NYC; nineteenth-century French fragmented **mirror**, CR-71; Civil War soldier's **bookcase**, Carla and Calvin Murphy @vividly.vintage; nineteenth-century **tea table**, Jason Counce @dirthomeandgardentn; 1940s steel Windsor **chair**, West Main Antiques, Barry Scales; vintage **rug**, Essy's Rug Gallery.

Memories Served Here: circa-1940s sawbuck **tables**, Country Living Fair, vendor Pam Bauer; **stools** repurposed from mill floor, CR-71; circa-1900s French art studio **chairs**, @peternappi; circa-1940s **rug**, Essy's Rug Gallery; nineteenth-century Bunnie's Place **sign** and **weathervane**, Jeremy Osborne, private picker; early 1900s **chopping block**, 2Storeys Antiques; nineteenth-century tin **birdhouse**, The Feathered Nest; stacked stoneware **bowls**, Lynda Hughes; primitive **wall cupboard**, Nashville Flea Market; 1950s wooden **bowls**, various thrift stores and vintage shows; handmade **cake stand**, @maisondemings; circa-1900s **dish cupboard**, The Nashville Show; Green Ridge Farm **restaurant ware**, Country Living Fair, vendor @southporch; 1960s pattern 1847 Rogers Bros. silver-plate **flatware**, my father Billy Miller, premium for car deal-erships for top sales **awards**; turkey **compote**, Our Thrift Store; nineteenth-century French **breadboards** and French **linens**, various vendors, Marburger Farm Antique Show.

The Gathering Place: nineteenth-century English **apothecary**, Winchester Antique Mall; Fourth of July styling (apothecary): **rug**, Essy's Rug Gallery; vintage **flag**, @judythill; unidenti-fied **flag collection**, private collector; nineteenth-century **horse fragment**, Country Living Fair, vendor @southporch; industrial floor **lamp**, @stcfinds; **chair**, Mitchell Gold + Bob Williams; slipcover, Annie McCreary @myswallowsnest; antique **rug**, Springfield Antiques

Show Extravaganza; circa-1940s wooden bank of **lockers**, Country Living Fair, vendor @gatheredcomforts; white pottery **bottle collection**, At Home; nineteenth-century **strong box**, The Nashville Show, vendor Kim Logan; vintage **portrait** of a gentleman, Nashville Flea Market, vendor Andy McRae; **soft goods**, At Home; antique **rug**, Essy's Rug Gallery.

Suite Dreams:
vintage French café **chalkboard**, The NAT Antiques and Collectibles; linen **duvet**, @roughlinen; nineteenth-century **chest on stand**, Winchester Antique Mall, vendor @scarlettscalesantiques; vintage New York Florist trade **sign**, Marburger Farm Antique Show, vendor @southporch; brass **deer**, Housing Works Thrift Shops, NYC; nineteenth-century **blanket chest**, 2Storeys Antiques; antique **rug**, Nashville Flea Market.

Once Upon a Dusty Old Attic: antique "Baptist Church" **sign**, Sheffield Antiques Mall; vintage "South" **road sign**, City Farmhouse Popup Fair, vendor @thecottonshed; repurposed scissor **lamps**, Marburger Farm Antique Show, vendor Eric Brown; antique **basket**, City Farmhouse Popup Fair, vendor La Petite Tresor; vintage **school table**, @scarlettscalesantiques; antique **chest of drawers**, addielanedesign.com; buffalo-check **chair**, At Home; vintage **string ball collection**, Nadine Brown Designs; vintage **mirror**, Nashville Flea Market, vendor Andy McRae; hand-stenciled **quilt pattern on board**, Katie Baker @baker_nest.

Vacancy: brass French hotel **bed**, Nashville Flea Market, vendor @lastlettervintage; vintage **side table**, GasLamp Antiques; vintage **portrait**, Nashville Flea Market;

vintage brass **candlesticks**, Our Thrift Store; Coloritto removable **wallpaper**, Boho Leaves, etsy.com/shop/Coloritto; vintage hotel **key cabinet**, private collection; vintage "Vacancy" **sign**, Winchester Antique Mall, vendor @inheritedandco; vintage **typewriter** and stand, Country Living Fair.

Double Play: nineteenth-century "Decorating" trade **sign**, Springfield Antiques Extravaganza; vintage **workbench**, Country Living Fair, vendor @gatheredcomforts; 1940s Mexican wedding **blanket**, GasLamp Antiques; "great catch" **oil on board**, private collection; vintage mud cloth **rugs**, **textiles**, Texas antiques week @hillcrestinnwarrenton.

CHAPTER 3— SHORT STORIES

A New Story for Collected Pieces: pointer dog kennel trade **sign**, Marburger Farm Antique Show, vendor @ vintagemercantile; nineteenth-century **apothecary**, Nashville Flea Market, vendor @lastlettervintage and @outlawantiques; primitive produce **table**, McKenzie Antique Mall; various **garden containers**, Nashville Flea Market, Country Living Fair; vintage lavender **basket**, Jason Counce @dirthomeandgardentn; Amish **apple picker**, ironstone barbershop **wash basin**, private collection; vintage **scale**, auction; nineteenth-century French **mattress stretchers**, Marburger Farm Antique Show, vendor @southporch; Victorian preserve **compotes**, Housing Works Thrift Shops, NYC; nineteenth-century clay **pie weights**, Ruth Barnes.

Trading Places: pair of tourist **portraits**, Chicago, Country Living Fair, vendor @cosmicgirlgoes; nineteenth-century Pennsylvania stoneware storage **jar**, Springfield Antiques Show Extravaganza; pair of French **confit jars**, La Bahia Antique Show, vendor @desirablejunk; artist Robert Witherspoon **oil on board**, Jeremy Osborne, private picker; vintage Cherokee basket, Antique Mall; circa-1930 medical **cabinet**, Brimfield Antique Shows; antique **stop sign**, private collection, Sheryl Crow; **accessories**, various thrift stores; dog **portrait**, The Village Antique and Home Décor Mall; fish **painting**, oil on canvas, Country Living Fair, vendor @cosmicgirlgoes; vintage studio **chair** and **easel**, McKenzie Antique Mall; nineteenth-century yellow-ware storage **jar**, Country Living Fair, vendor Five Corners Antique.

The Art of a Storied Display: nineteenth-century **barn floor**, Heart of Ohio Antique Center; **portrait** "Laguna Surfer," GasLamp Antiques; rustic **cupboard**, Ohio Valley Antique Mall; vintage California yacht **flag**, Marburger Farm Antique Show, vendor @throughtheporthole; vintage rummage sale **sign**, @hillcrestinnwarrenton Texas antiques week, field pick; vintage **clothing**, flannel shirts, Housing Works Thrift Shops, NYC; 1940s French laborer's **jacket**, Levi's **jacket**, Marburger Farm Antique Show, vendor @qualitymending; vintage shop **cabinet**, private collection; nineteenth-century **hook/coat board**, Country Living Fair, vendor Five Corners Antiques; vintage **toy camper**, gift, private collection, Gina Gann; New York Cotton Exchange **trading chart**, Ohio Valley Antique Mall; vintage **ledger**, GasLamp Antiques; tinted photographs of a woman, GasLamp Antiques; vintage and antique letters, various thrift stores and flea markets; nineteenth-century French hanging apothecary, Lynda Hughes; nineteenth-century cabinet cards, various flea markets and thrift shops; vintage coat rack, Nashville Flea Market; folk-art make-do nineteenth-century country chair, Antique Mall; postal holiday closure sign, @antiques_horseshoe_ben; antique mailbox, private collection.

CHAPTER 4— A STORY FOR ALL SEASONS

Shown in each season: nineteenth-century calendar blackboard, South Road Antiques.

Page 174–175: vintage seascape, Nashville Flea Market, vendor Rodney and Carol Logan.

Spring: nineteenth-century Swedish demilune table, @campdavidinteriors; vintage theater chair, CR-71; vintage black-and-white quilt, Country Living Fair, vendor @cosmicgirlgoes; vintage metal bunny basket, Nashville Flea Market; vintage cement garden bunny, The Gilded Sparrow; vintage stone paver repurposed as tray, Flying Miz Daisy, vendor Cascas Vintage and Design.

Summer: set of four vintage Woodard garden chairs, Country Living Fair, vendor @cosmicgirlgoes; nineteenth-century farm table, City Farmhouse Popup Fair, vendor Carla and Calvin Murphy @vividly.vintage; vintage bucket, Marburger Farm Antique Show, vendor @jbsmercantile; folk-art oil on board of a country church, City Farmhouse Popup Fair, vendor Carla and Calvin Murphy @vividly.vintage; nineteenth-century country mantel, @velvetsvintageantiques; "County Fair" sign, Country Living Fair, vendor Five Corners Antiques; nineteenth-century grain bucket, Country Living Fair, vendor @jbsmercantile; nineteenth-century apothecary drawers, Sweet Salvage, vendor @vindustrial_supply_co; vintage ice cream bucket, The Nashville Show; honeymoon art, gift, singer/songwriter Kim Carnes; nineteenth-century bucket bench, Ohio Valley Antique

Mall; **oil on canvas**, Oregon beachscape, Flying Miz Daisy.

Fall: vintage Spode dessert **plates**, Spring Hill Antique Mall; vintage handmade **flowerpot**, Nashville Flea Market; extra-large French **grain scoop**, Flying Miz Daisy, vendor Cascas Vintage and Design; vintage Campbell's Soup **mugs**, Ohio Valley Antique Mall.

Winter: 1940s book **illustrations** from 1826 schoolbook, Country Living Fair, vendor @roseandgracemarket; twentieth-century **patent renderings**, Country Living Fair; vintage **pitcher**, Nashville Flea Market; primitive wall **cupboard** with **Santa mugs**, Nashville Flea Market; hand-painted **Christmas tree art**, gift, Melissa Cervantes @dumpsterdiva1923;

original art, acrylic on canvas snowman, gift, Lila Taylor; circa-1940s handmade **chandelier**, @scarlettscalesantiques; vintage original painted **church window**, McKenzie Antique Mall; handmade **Christmas trees** repurposed from barn doors, Country Living Fair, vendor @southporch.

ANTIQUE SHOWS AND FLEA MARKETS

BRIMFIELD ANTIQUE SHOWS
May, July, and September
For complete show listings,
dates, and times, visit
brimfieldshow.org

CITY FARMHOUSE POPUP FAIR AND POPUP SHOPS
Franklin, Tennessee 37064
cityfarmhousefranklin.com
Instagram: @cityfarmhouse
Refer to website or Instagram
for schedule

COUNTRY LIVING FAIR
fair.countryliving.com
Refer to website for schedule

FLYING MIZ DAISY
California—various locations
flyingmizdaisy.com
Instagram: @flyingmizdaisy
Seasonal
Refer to website for schedule

MARBURGER FARM ANTIQUE SHOW
2248 Texas 237
Round Top, Texas 78954
roundtop-marburger.com
Spring and Fall

NASHVILLE FLEA MARKET
500 Wedgewood Ave.
Nashville, Tennessee 37203
thefairgrounds.com/fleamarket
Monthly

THE NASHVILLE SHOW
Tennessee State Fairgrounds
625 Smith Ave.
Nashville, Tennessee 37203
thenashvilleshowantiques.com
February

SPRINGFIELD ANTIQUES EXTRAVAGANZA
Clark County Fairgrounds
4401 S. Charleston Pike
Springfield, Ohio 45505
springfieldantiqueshow.com
May, September

SWEET SALVAGE
4648 7th Ave.
Phoenix, Arizona 85013
sweetsalvage.net
Monthly every third weekend
Thursday–Sunday

TEXAS ANTIQUES WEEK
roundtop.org
Spring and Fall
Refer to website for shows and
schedules

ANTIQUE MALLS

ANTIQUE MALL
1386 Wears Valley Rd.
Pigeon Forge, Tennessee 37863
865-908-3222

GASLAMP ANTIQUES & DECORATING MALL
GasLamp Too
100 and 128 Powell Place,
Suite 200
Nashville, Tennessee 37204
615-297-2224
615-292-2250

HEARTLAND ANTIQUES AND COLLECTIBLES
1441 Winfield Dunn Pkwy.
Sevierville, Tennessee 37876
865-429-1791

HEART OF OHIO ANTIQUE CENTER
4785 E. National Rd.
Springfield, Ohio 45505
937-324-2188

MCKENZIE ANTIQUE MALL
14890 Highland Dr.
McKenzie, Tennessee 38201
731-352-9344

THE NAT ANTIQUES AND
   COLLECTIBLES
2705 SW 6th Ave.
Amarillo, Texas 79106
806-367-8908
thenatroute66.com

OHIO VALLEY ANTIQUE MALL
7285 Dixie Hwy.
Fairfield, Ohio 45014
513-874-7855

SHEFFIELD ANTIQUES MALL
684 W. Poplar Ave.
Collierville, Tennessee 38017
901-853-7822

SPRING HILL ANTIQUE MALL
1213 School St.
Spring Hill, Tennessee 37174
931-489-0022
springhillantiques.com
Instagram:
@thespringhillantiquemall

THE VILLAGE ANTIQUE AND
   HOME DÉCOR MALL
1442 Winfield Dunn Pkwy.
Sevierville, Tennessee 37876
865-366-2348

WINCHESTER ANTIQUE MALL
121 2nd Ave. N.
Franklin, Tennessee 37064
615-791-5846

ANTIQUE SHOPS

2STOREYS ANTIQUES
2983 Carter's Creek Station Rd.
Columbia, Tennessee 38401
931-446-7090
 2storeysantiques.net
Instagram: @2storeys

ABLES ANTIQUES
Kitty and Tony Ables
By appointment: 731-772-5638
Instagram: @kitty_brackin_

CITY FARMHOUSE
117 Third Ave., N.
Franklin, Tennessee 37064
615-268-0216
cityfarmhousefranklin.com
@cityfarmhouse

CR-71
Located in the Factory at
Franklin
230 Franklin Rd.
Franklin, Tennessee 37064
615-715-8120
Instagram: @cr71biz

ENEBYHOME
Doug and Carina Jenkins
Enebyhome.com
Online or by warehouse appt.
info@enebyhome.com
404-512-40017
Instagram: @enebyhome

THE FEATHERED NEST
Larry and Tina Kauffman
772 CR 1150 E.
Sullivan, Illinois 61951
217-254-8894
Instagram: @thefeatherednest1

THE GILDED SPARROW
219 N. Range Ave.
Denham Springs, Louisiana
70726
225-369-2632
thegildedsparrow.net
Instagram: @thegildedsparrow

LYNDA HUGHES
Lynda Hughes Primitives and
American Country
By appointment: 770-546-4088
Email: lysuhug@live.com
Instagram: @lysuhug

SOUTH ROAD ART AND
   ANTIQUES
By appointment
southroadantiques.com
Instagram: @southroadantiques

WEST MAIN ANTIQUES
1182 West Main St.
Franklin, Tennessee 37064
615-614-3392

THRIFT STORES

HOUSING WORKS THRIFT SHOPS
Located in New York City and
Brooklyn, New York
For store locations,
visit housingworks.org

OUR THRIFT STORE
1018 Columbia Ave.
Franklin, Tennessee 37064
615-591-9612
Instagram: @ourthriftstore

UNIQUE BOUTIQUE
1674 Third Ave.
New York, New York 10128
212-828-8900

URBAN THRIFTER
A side hustle of the City
Farmhouse brand
Located inside the
Spring Hill Antique Mall
1213 School St.
Spring Hill, Tennessee 37174
615-268-0216
cityfarmhousefranklin.com
Instagram: @cityfarmhouse

HOME GOODS

FLOWER FARMER
Natchez-Glen
4117 New Hwy 96 W
Franklin, Tennessee 37064
You pick or ship, flower growing
classes on site or online
natchezglen.com

FURNITURE
Mitchell Gold + Bob Williams
mgbwhome.com

RUGS
Essy's Rug Gallery
324 Liberty Pike #150
Franklin, Tennessee 37064
615-595-0959
essysruggallery.com

PILLOWS
At Home
Locations nationwide
athome.com (for locations and
online ordering)

LINENS, BEDCOVERINGS, TABLE COVERINGS, AND MORE
Rough Linen
roughlinen.com (online ordering)

CHAPTER 2— OTHER PEOPLE'S STORIES

Curious as to where my Franklin friends who are featured in "Other People's Stories" (page 62) love to shop? Seems as though they keep it local. Here are the lists and Instagram links to local Franklin and Nashville favorites.

Some are previously listed under Antique Malls.

The Barn Door Co. @thebarndoorco (Franklin)

City Farmhouse @cityfarmhouse (Franklin)

CR-71 @cr71biz (Franklin)

Franklin Antique Mall @franklinantiquemall (Franklin)

The Iron Gate @theirongate (Franklin and Nashville)

The Pick-it Fence @thepickitfence (Leiper's Fork)

Preservation Station @preservationstation (Nashville)

Props Antiques @propsantiques (Leiper's Fork)

T. Nesbitt & Co. @t.nesbittandco (Franklin)

Winchester Antique Mall @winchester_antiques (Franklin)

FAVORITE PICKING SPOTS FROM "SHORT STORIES: PEN PALS" (PAGE 160)

Ruth Barnes
Ruth claims to shop mostly her own home and digs from the yard (she claims the price tags are easier on her pocketbook).

SOUTHERN VINTAGE CO.
4210 Altruria Rd.
Bartlett, Tennessee 38135
901-832-8292
southernvintageco.com
Instagram: @southernvintageco

Jen Hamilton
MONTICELLO ANTIQUE MARKETPLACE
8600 SE Stark St.
Portland, Oregon 97216
503-256-8600
monticelloantiques.com

BARTON ANTIQUE MALL
25618 SE Highway 224
Boring, Oregon 97009
503-637-3300
bartonantiquemall.com

Jane Peet
THE DEPOT AT GIBSON MILL
325 McGill Ave., NW
Concord, North Carolina 28026
704-787-9351

Becki Griffin
BAYBERRY ANTIQUES
12408 E. Texas St.
Burton, Texas 77835
956-393-7151

OLD GLORY ANTIQUES
206 South Washington
Round Top, Texas 78954
720-435-1482

Anne Karp
Anne stalks the website estatesales.net to find local sales. It's where she finds her beloved buttons. Here is a list of her favorite store haunts.

GOLDEN NUGGET ANTIQUE
    FLEA MARKET
1850 River Rd. / Route 29
Lambertville, New Jersey
08530
gnflea.com

THE SUMMIT ANTIQUES
    CENTER
511 Morris Ave.
Summit, New Jersey 07901
908-273-9373
thesummitantiquescenter.com

Catherine Pierce
MOUNTAIN HOME ANTIQUES
6582 Rte. 191
Cresco, Pennsylvania 18326
570-595-8581

THE FACTORY ANTIQUES
130 W. Main St.
Silverdale, Pennsylvania 18962
215-453-1414

ISBAELLA SPARROW
8433 Germantown Ave.
Chestnut Hill, Pennsylvania
19002
717-327-7285

SHOPPING TRIPS

If you don't have time to
plan a pick on your own, my
friend Suzie Stroup puts
together the most amaz-
ing friends' getaways. No
detail is left to chance, from
the stunning homes that
she books for the stay to
the five-star restaurants,
catered meals, and gor-
geously decorated parties.
It's a glamourous way to
satisfy your passion for
picking.

BEAUTIFUL ADVENTURES
    —LUXURY GIRLFRIEND
    GETAWAYS
Suzie Stroup
Black Sheep Flea Designs
blacksheepflea.com
Instagram: @blacksheepflea

STAY HERE

THE BIG BLUE HOUSE
    (PAGE 74)
Leiper's Fork
community of Franklin,
Tennessee
When Jamie is out visiting
family and friends in sunny
Malibu, she turns the Big Blue
House into a vacation rental.
It's a glorious place to stay
in the country, and the house
offers plenty of room for a
girlfriends' weekend or a big
family reunion. If you plan on
a getaway to the area, I highly
recommend that you stay
here.
For reservations: vrbo.com/
927617 or directly via
Instagram at
@houseandsanctuary

SUGAR SHACK (PAGE 82)
Walking distance from historic
downtown Franklin, Tennessee
For history buffs and Main
Street shoppers, book your
stay in the coziest cottage in
town. When Harrison and John
decided to share their home
with family and friends, I was
first on the list even though
I live here! It's perfect for a
couple looking for a romantic
place to call home for a weekend (or longer).
For reservations: vrbo.com/
1075689

ABOUT THE AUTHOR

Kim Leggett is the author of the best-selling book, *City Farmhouse Style* (2017), an interior designer, and antiques and vintage dealer. She and her husband, David, own City Farmhouse, Urban Thrifter, and the City Farmhouse Pop-up Fairs. Kim was named one of the Country's 100 Most Creative People by *Country Living* magazine, and a Style Maker by *Country Home* magazine. She received the prestigious Urban Land Institute Award for Excellence in Design for her work at Homestead Manor in Thompson Station, Tennessee.

Kim's design work has been featured in *Country Living*, *Country Home*, *Architectural Digest* online, and numerous other publications.

cityfarmhousefranklin.com

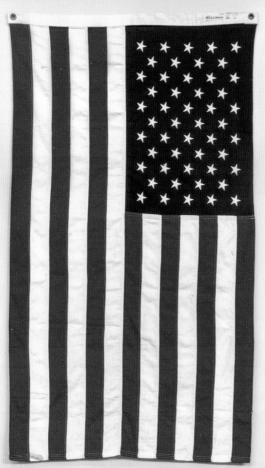

It was a "Why I Love America" essay contest that inspired me to tell the story of Old Glory in my bedroom at the ripe old age of eight. Sponsored by the local Dyersburg Women's Club, and similar organizations throughout Tennessee and forty-nine states, the award for each winner was a flag flown over the White House in Washington, D.C. I was honored to have been selected as the winner representing my home state and elementary school, Jennie Bell. I brought the flag home and hung it above my bed. All who came to visit got the full story, not just once, but many times thereafter. Let's say I was a little proud to tell it.

ACKNOWLEDGMENTS

Writing a book is not for the lonely. It takes a village of family, friends, creatives, cheerleaders, and a strong relationship with God. For all of you who were alongside me, I am forever grateful.

The Planner and Architect . . . God, so many times I wondered where we were going with this, but you never failed to bring me home.

The Builder . . . ABRAMS, and the amazing and always patient Abrams Team: my editor Shawna Mullen, designer Sebit Min, creative director Deb Wood, design manager Danielle Youngsmith, managing editor Glenn Ramirez, and production manager Alison Gervais.

The Angel . . . Lila Taylor, who through your talent at the young age of fourteen, closed many paragraphs when I had nothing left in me. Please grow up to be a writer. You have a huge talent!

The Chief Cook, Bottle Washer, and Man of the House . . . David, without you this would have never happened. I know you are exhausted.

The Picture Takers . . . Leslie Brown, you brought my stories to life beautifully! Cami Bradley and Allison Olszewski, such amazing talent for capturing color!

The Family . . . Ruth Barnes, P.J. Dempsey, and Fifi O'Neill, sisters from another mother. You know me, you understand me, and that week you talked me off the ledge will go down in the history books.

The Friends . . . Katie and Randy Williams, Jamie Parsons, Harrison Houlé and John Schuck, Laura and Daniel M., Annie and Darryl McCreary, Jenni and Jared Bowlin, Doug and Carina Jenkins, and Celeste Shaw-Coulston, I'm so honored to have y'all as friends. Thank you for allowing me to show the world your gorgeous homes and tell your stories.

The Pen Pals . . . Ruth Barnes, Jen Hamilton, Jane Peet, Becki Griffin, Anne Karp, and Catherine Pierce. Who would have known that our friendship would have blossomed behind those tiny little squares?

The Team . . . Jason Counce, Georgie Daniel, and Ruth Barnes, I called and you all always came. Love you all! Steve Mydelski, my guy for dahlias (I swear you were out there with a heat lamp getting them to bloom); Steve McLellan, my guy for flowers that aren't in season. It's in the details!

The Cheerleaders . . . Suzie Stroup, Jenni McCadams, and Lyndee Stevens, I am forever grateful for your encouragement and love throughout this journey. You three made me believe in myself when I thought I had lost my mind.

Ya'll, we did it!!!! xoxoxo

EDITOR:
Shawna Mullen

DESIGNER:
Sebit Min

PRODUCTION MANAGER:
Alison Gervais

Library of Congress
Control Number: 2020931038

ISBN: 978-1-4197-4738-0
eISBN: 978-1-64700-020-2

Text copyright © 2020
Kim Leggett

Cover © 2020 Abrams

PHOTO CREDITS:
Pages 96–101: Hideout, Ruby and
Peach Photo; pages 114–119: Boldly
Stated, Cami Bradley Photography;
page 149: Leanna Koesy-Wood;
pages 160 and 163: Sentimental
Style, Becki Griffin; page 166–167:
Trail Blazers, Jen Hamilton; page
168: Signs of Home, Jane Peet;
pages 170–171: The Button Picker,
Jessica Reiss; page 173: In Search
of a Country Cupboard, Catherine
Pierce; pages 191 and 197: Ruth
Barnes.

All other photographs, copyright
© 2020 Leslie Brown.

Printed and bound in China
10 9 8 7 6 5 4 3 2

Abrams books are available at
special discounts when purchased
in quantity for premiums and
promotions as well as fundraising
or educational use. Special
editions can also be created to
specification. For details, contact
specialsales@abramsbooks.com or
the address below.

Abrams® is a registered
trademark of
Harry N. Abrams, Inc.

ABRAMS The Art of Books
195 Broadway, New York, NY 10007
abramsbooks.com